# VERY A
# DRIVING

## PUBLISHER'S NOTE

Tom Topper's earlier book (uniform with this one) "Learning to Drive in Pictures", was acclaimed by "The Times", "The Daily Telegraph", "The Sketch", "The Sun", "The Daily Mirror", "Woman's Own" and others.

It is used in hundreds of Driving Schools and in an increasing number of colleges where youngsters are learning the theory before reaching test age.

The sales quickly exceeded 6 figures and more publicity was accorded when the 2nd edition appeared by the "Daily Mail", London's "Evening News" and "Woman's Own" (again).

We offer a *money back guarantee* if a reader fails his test *or* does not agree it is the world's best book on learning to drive. We have had no claims up to the time of writing.

# VERY ADVANCED DRIVING

BY

## A. TOM. TOPPER

# PAPERFRONTS

## ELLIOT RIGHT WAY BOOKS
## KINGSWOOD, SURREY, U.K.

Made and printed in Great Britain by
C. Nicholls & Company Ltd.
and published by
Elliot Right Way Books
Kingswood, Surrey, U.K.

# *Contents*

turning right onto a road with two lanes each way. Zebra crossing safety. Headlight flashing. Headlight flashing customs. Traffic light knowledge. Use Green Efficiently. Going fast through green on wide empty "through" routes. One-ways. First example of the advantages of using the lane least likely to be held up. One-way underpasses. Second example of using the lane least likely to be held up. Multilane city roundabouts. Third example of using the lane least likely to be held up. The "road narrows" problem. Approaching one-way streets. Traffic flow. Easy-way for one-ways. Town streets. How a signal can banish doubt. Do you always look under parked cars? Hooting on behalf of others. Swarming pedestrians. Hidden monsters. Blind spots. Systemizing a safety eye approach to junctions. The deadly blind corner. The danger of stalling. A trick which is naughty, but nice. Positioning-safety's supreme ally. Stopping and parking. Pedestrians are crackers. Motto for reversing—don't.

## 4. COUNTRY TECHNIQUES 84

Our smaller country roads. Really narrow lanes. Roads just wide enough for two cars. Crossroads in country lanes. Main roads crossing the countryside. Leaving room for others to overtake. The nightmare three lanes, two way. Bends to the Right. Bends to the left. Disappearing Gap. Double white lines, Herring bone lines. Where side roads cross main ones. How it may be possible to save time when you join a main road. Villages out in country routes. Talking and looking at the countryside. "Guesswork" navigation. Summary of policy.

## 5. OVERTAKING 96

Reduce time exposure to danger. Preparatory eyework. An example of preparation. Example of preparation at Right Hand Curve. What happens if he pulls out? What to do if things go wrong when you are committed to and nearly past a car. "Balance". "Directional confidence". Textbooks frighten people about cutting in. Overtaking principle for three lane two-way roads. Follow my leader overtaking. The world of difference between an accelerating pass and passing with speed in hand. Telling Someone in front he should have the chance to pass first. "Prison". The Russian roulette pass.

## 6 BAD WEATHER 109

Fog. Surprise Patches of Fog. Spitting Rain. What to do. Cloudbursts, torrential rain. Overtaking in rain. Sunshine. Dazzle in the mirror. When dazzled yourself.

## 7. NIGHT DRIVING 113

Twilight or dawn, or poor light. In towns. Helping people at junctions. More tips for town at night. Following other people. In the country. When leading a stream through the countryside. The permanently dipped or "Dippy" driver. Passing cyclists or small obstructions at night. Speed in the dark. Dazzling. Overtaking at night. A passing headache. Extra risks overtaking at night. Signals for night-time overtaking. Odd night time tips. Dim lights.

# LIST OF ILLUSTRATIONS

9

# Watch for the catch in Advanced Driving!

Long before people talked about "advanced" driving my publishers brought out a book in two parts one of which dealt with "The Advanced Driver". The term *advanced driver* is now used widely.

Various courses and competitions give "passes" for "special ability". To obtain such "qualifications" can cost a lot of money and in my view they are hardly worth the paper on which they are written.

Unfortunately, it is certain that the motive of many in getting these "passes" is the hope that others—including the insurance companies, some employers, and the courts—will think because they have the pass they are expert drivers. I am sure this does not fool many magistrates or our great British judges.

I fear that many who go after these passes imagine themselves to be "road Gods", superior to all the other, silly drivers, than which there is nothing more dangerous. The late Lady Attlee, wife of the former Socialist Prime Minister got her "pass" yet subsequently succeeded in having a great many accidents. I am sorry to criticise the dead but it is a good example of the humbug of it all. I have been passenger with a number of "certified" drivers who have scared the life out of me.

## Diploma Mania

We live in an age in which people have become obsessed by diplomas and bits of paper, yet everyone from the day they pass the simple government test should be learning to drive better by experience and the study of driving. That is what matters and not being able to swank some certificate or other. Nothing must be allowed (even unconsciously) to come before SAFETY and THOUGHTFULNESS for other road users.

## Mind Preparation

My aim is to encourage *you* to think about and analyse your own driving, and to develop continuing enthusiasm for safe,

11

happy motoring. "Very" advanced driving is largely common-sense based on safety for others and self preservation. But such commonsense has to be reflected upon, chewed over in the mind, if it is to become "common" and automatic on to-day's appallingly dangerous roads. You need to train your mind to meet emergencies, for only if knowledge and experience have become a part of your subconscious, will you have the ability, *on which lives may depend*, to react correctly and quickly enough during split second unexpected emergencies. It is the mind preparation–learning from and thinking about your experiences—that makes the right reaction "instinctive".

## Positioning And Speed

Not all the boffins in Whitehall, not all the clauses in the Highway Code, nor the whole lot of "passes" or driving certificates, speed limits, police cars and road engineers put together with anything else you like, can equal in importance the twin points which are so rarely stressed—*positioning and relating speed to conditions*.

Neither the one nor the other can save you, but the use of the both at once is the basis of the very advanced driving which this book attempts to explain.

# I

# "Buppy Drivers"

Many dead drivers would be living had they not stopped learning and thinking for themselves at driving test standard. Becoming "very" advanced is a personal challenge requiring continual and concentrated thinking effort.

## WHAT IS A BUPPY DRIVER MUMMY?

"The Buppy people" first bounced into this world in Roy Neal's masterpiece called "Make Money In A Shop" (Paperfront series). By definition they are the customers who buy by price and appearance only. They do not possess sufficient intelligence to buy by quality or functional ability, but blindly follow the dictates of the Ad-men. Roy Neal has revealed how to profit from the multitude of Buppy people . . . *here* we use them to sound dread warnings . . . I am indebted to this wonderful book for the use of the word Buppy. It is a bible for retailers and wholesalers.

"Buppy" people ever conform with conformity, that is they copy each other and strive to do the approved or accepted thing. Rarely, if ever, do they think for themselves. "Buppies" may not all conform with each other, but they usually fall into clearly defined groups. Thus stockbrokers with their pinstriped suits, bowler hats, furled umbrellas and buttonholes are as "Buppy" as are "The Bingo Brigade", another group.

There are millions of Buppy motorists. I will indicate a few types:

### The Jealous Buppy

He accelerates when being overtaken and slows up when he's not, seemingly doing everything he can to hold up other peoples' progress.

### The Wandering Mind Or Erratic Buppy

He weaves along thinking about anything but what he is

doing and often makes abrupt stops when he hasn't noticed something in time. Some are erratic, plunging to the depths of sluggardliness at times, but expect them to be going "flat out" the next minute.

### The Nervy Ones

They are abominably slow and apparently unable to digest what is happening around them. They may not realise in some instances or want to know how much anger builds up in the queue behind.

### The "My Speed" Type

These Buppies have a set speed at which happiness overcomes them. It varies not whether conditions are safe or a dangerous shopping area is at hand. Relentlessly they maintain "their" speed, holding up faster people on open roads perhaps, but worse, a threat to life whenever they pass through crowded areas.

### The Motorway "My Speed" Buppy

I quote from a Roy Neal letter on this subject.

"The Buppy People follow Anybody, Anything. They *have* to follow somebody or something, otherwise they'd get stuck on the hard shoulder, having no initiative of their own. . . .

"Friday night on the M.1. is merciless example. Friday night, contrary to the B.B.C's impression, is *not* music night, it's b eeting mad Buppies night as thousands of week-end commuters are spewn from London in nose-to-tail escape to country freedom.

"Ever been in a multiple pile-up? Odds are that if you use the M.1. northways on a Friday night—yes. There's more such pile-ups than ever reach a bye-line in the Muck-Binding Echo, let alone headlines in the national press.

"Twenty cars up ahead you can see the first glow of red brake lights. Sensibly you ease your own brakes on slowly, then quickly, as the column in front crunches to a halt.

"Unfortunately . . . somebody behind you has not been noticing those red lights . . . or else he thought it was a mobile knocking shop maybe? Either way, the upshot is that he cannot stop as quick as you can. *If* you are lucky, then he'll manage to swivel into the central reservation and come to a halt lower down. If you ain't lucky, then pass this book on to somebody else, you won't be needing it.

"When it happened to me—there were *three* cars came up the central reservation. Each one was an old banger! They just hadn't got the brakes to match the situation! Fact. It happened. So what the Hell were the three drivers doing in the fast lane bumper to bumper, with brakes that didn't stop so good?

"70 m.p.h.

"That's what.

"Talk about Buppy Drivers! It must have taken each driver up to half an hour apiece to pump their old crocks up to the said 70 m.p.h. Then they proceeded to stay in the fast lane. They couldn't have thought what they were doing . . . they must have just blindly followed their leaders—any bloody leader who happened to be handy???

"It ain't no secret that you should drive according to prevailing conditions is it? Does it have to be printed in black and white that the condition of the car counts as well?"

## Good Drivers (Possibly "Very" Advanced Buppies!)

A man who speeds through a space having 1″ clearance to his left (but several feet to the right) may be superb—or a B . . . F . . . ! (Regrettably probably the latter.) You judge people as you follow. The good ones rarely weave or dart side to side; braking is infrequent and turning round to talk taboo. Following, you feel secure that they will warn of any problem and you can guess their reaction in difficulty. "Slow in danger, get moving when it's clear" is their motto.

In the mirror you will notice the good never weave, especially police cars! During danger they fall noticeably *further* back, only coming close when there may be a possible overtaking opportunity. You can often tell if a Police car is following by the way it is driven.

## Other Good Drivers

The twenty ton lorry, cement mixer or the vintage Bentley will rarely hit you—these drivers are professionals—BEWARE the ten year old family car, local grocery van and the young speed-merchant in his racer! Watch the learner out for the first day who will likely jam on the brakes if the gear stick shakes! The "very" advanced driver will wish to avoid being identified with a non-thinking BUPPY group, though he might admit to being a "very" advanced Buppy!—at least a "Thinking Buppy", not "Buppy Buppy"!

The thinking (advanced-"Buppy") driver continually plans his advanced positioning methods as traffic problems dictate. I stress this because for all I know, *you* could still have "Buppy" Buppy ideas. It may require courage and the eating of "humble pie" to drop "Buppy" habits and to honestly analyse where you are right and when wrong. *To guard against having irrevocably set ideas* for this or that situation, a CONTINUING review is essential. New better methods MUST be allowed freedom to emerge.

With decisions made instantly during driving, sometimes hardest of all is stopping oneself acting knowingly wrongly, i.e., taking chances. Only self-control prevents you and if it is not your strong personal point, it will likely be your driving weakness. Answer—put yourself right and your driving will accord. Self-discipline is the scarcest, yet most essential good driving ingredient.

## SLOW DOWN BY 10%

Here is an eye opener. Next time you drive, cut usual speeds by 10% and keep your eyes flashing, trying to watch every danger possibility. You will probably be staggered that you were ever accident free at previous higher speeds, even if you did not think yourself a fast driver.

## RUNNING COMMENTARY

Running a commentary out loud about where danger lurks, why and how you are counteracting each risk helps you to think more deliberately. Passengers, if any, may learn too. Example:

### Home To Half Way To The Office—Distance One Mile

". . . the momentum from this burst of acceleration should carry us up the drive as far as the gate so that we reach it at barely rolling speed. I do this to allow time to watch for kids running on the grass verge outside our fence because only when I know this first danger is clear dare I move the car out to the edge of the road. Then I always look right *first* because even up our quiet hill cars come fast and close to the grass.

"Now I'm gathering clutch control and holding a finger on the choke as I look right and left. With a cold engine that's vital to prevent stalling half way out. All clear! So, off we go and I'm making an *immediate* check in the mirror as we straighten up. Wow! here's a fastard behind already. I'm moving in to let him pass and keeping a special eye on the Browns' gateway as I am not usually this close.

"Towards the bottom of the hill I shall use 2nd gear for engine braking keeping me well in control for our left turn into the road that crosses. There's a new fastard in the mirror now so I'm giving him extra brake light flashes to warn him we may have to stop at the bottom. He's 'pushing' me already and this makes me doubt if he realises how fast drivers swish from the right at the T-join.

"Good, we're clear, so he's lucky too. On this narrow bit I'm keeping well to the middle and watching all the driveways because people reverse out—especially being the rush hour. At the top where the road crosses and we turn right to go down the hill I have to hug the left because our road is so bottle-necked. If you don't you make it impossible for people to turn into this road—and it's usually your best friend's wife coming back from the station just down the hill who gets caught! There's another catch at this turn because of this silly fence on the left that masks our view of anyone coming. I do the same 'roll stop' technique here (as at my gate) because you quite often get some late blighter who's running down to catch the train, dive right across the bonnet. I suppose if you didn't know the area at least the tell-tale pavement edge would give you some clue! You have to show sympathy . . . and care.

"You can see further to the right here than you can to the left so I always look left *last* before and as we pull out. Right, it's clear, off we go! Mirror check. Nothing there. That fellow behind's had to wait because of this van coming up the hill. 2nd, 3rd, this is fast enough. I'm covering the brake already in case that chap waiting in the side road to the left hasn't seen us yet. He's not looking our way. I'm slowing the car instinctively—watching for swerving options—there's still no-one behind—hoot to warn—GOODNESS! STOP! Would you believe anyone could pull out like that. Glad I suspected him!

"Now we go on over this bridge and take left at the cross-roads. I started to assess the crossroads immediately I reached the top of the bridge, as they came into view. You can see from there what's coming from the right and if there's anyone from straight ahead, or if its clear, as it is this morning. This helps you get time to watch the hidden latch gate on the corner on our left. You can just see it now. I swing fairly wide of it if I can, like to-day because some young children live there.

"Now this **S** bend we are coming to needs care because there is a long straight at its far end and approaching drivers might misjudge their speed while entering it. It looks slightly damp on the first bit of the bend so I'm keeping her slow, not accelerating at all. Notice how I'm hugging my own side. There won't be much time if someone comes skidding towards me this wet morning!

"No marks for hard acceleration on this straight while the engine is still cold so I take it easy. 3rd gear as we pass this trunk road sign normally slows me just right for stopping when we reach the main road.

"Turning left here it is essential to look left *last*—BEFORE moving! What happens is you drive up and stop as we are now and look right. Say that it is clear. So you look left. A steady stream is on its way into town but, you think, they need not affect my left turn. So you look right. Still clear, say. Do you go? . . . NO SIR! because while you are sitting here waiting you can bet your life a fastard will pop out of the stream from the left and start overtaking the others. One move from you and you're dead!

"So, it's clear right and I'm looking left last. Today seems to be the exception—the're all behaving and we can go. I'm accelerating briskly because traffic catches up behind so fast if you dawdle. I keep a finger at the ready on the headlight flasher all the way along here because this road has a peculiar width which seems to encourage people to try and 'force' a deadly third middle lane and there isn't room. There's one poking out from behind that lorry. Ah! he's seen my flash.

"I'm easing off for the crossroads coming up 'DESPITE' give way markings against crossing traffic—covering the brake too. I find that pays, especially in rush hour when people waiting get more impatient. . . ."

## THINK WITH THE "OTHER" DRIVER

*Consideration for others is the essence of good driving manners.*
Each road "reading" can have different implications for a lorry
driver, a sports car man, a pedestrian or a pram pusher. Put
absurdly, the same gap that is a headache to a ten tonner is
chicken feed to a cyclist. But a steep hill which buckles a
cyclist's knees is whizzed up by an empty truck. One needs to
link consciousness of others' problems with *thought* and that
means effort!

CONSIDERING "his" viewpoint, you then . . . do all
possible to HELP him, moving over, closing up, stopping or
as appropriate.

## JOIN "CANNONBALL" IN THE HOT SEAT

Readers may remember the Cannonball adventures on tele-
vision glorifying the sweat of long distance heavy lorry, heavy
responsibility, work. I recently had the pleasure and honour of
working and driving with "big lorry" boys and specially thank
my friends John Wales, Gordon, Tom, Gerry, Terry and Les,
all of Express Deliveries, London N.17. My purpose was so
that I could illustrate for you how you can "think with" the
lorry driver.

### Their Pet Hates

1) Buppy Parkers near narrow street ends, depot entrances
or other turn-ins who prevent them getting round.

2) Overtakers who immediately slow down. On a heavily
loaded wagon with six or eight gears and a heavy clutch, being
forced to go down and up the gearbox is good reason to be
furious! It's more exercise than most people take in a week!
Allow heavy vehicles to maintain speed and forget priority
rights where you can make way for them on uphills. You ease
it for them and all behind them.

3) Drivers following who see the lorry's difficulty in entering
a narrow street but still close up leaving them no reversing
space. Don't or you may get squashed!

If a "big" boy is pulling from a narrow street into your
road, also of narrow width, his rear wheels have to cut the
corner. Position well back (Fig. 1) to ease his task.

**How to Help Them**

1) Hoot on overtaking, when near enough to penetrate cab noises. Sports cars especially are not easily seen from high cabs.

2) You may see a "big" boy reversing unaided about to touch something hidden from his mirror; give rapid or long hoots to denote anguish and to alert.

3) Lorry drivers, when *they overtake you*, appreciate a headlamp flash telling it is safe to come in. With 60 feet body-work this is hard to judge. With danger perhaps appearing ahead (unseen by the *overtaken* driver beyond the lorry), the signal may avert a smash.

### "THINK WITH" THE SPORTS DRIVERS

Well balanced powerful sports cars may reach 70 m.p.h. in *less than half* the time of a family saloon. Driven rightly, such cars overtake safely on short clear stretches while others in a traffic procession dare not contemplate trying. To enhance this safety the "very advanced" family car driver ensures he *is* leaving room wherever possible for the sports machine to zip past safely. Chapter 11 discusses fast driving.

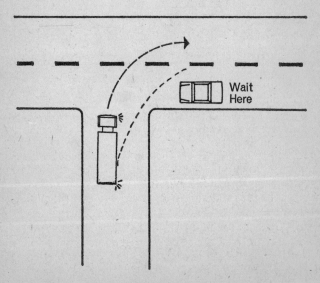

Fig. 1. Waiting well back for a lorry to emerge.

## MOTORBIKE OR MORGUE?

*Statistically your chance of dying in a motorcycle crash is nearly twenty times your risk in a car—as is your chance of crashing.*

Braking and steering control are greatly inferior. Their massive acceleration can also be deadly for the inexperienced or undisciplined.

Realization of these FACTS counts. Know from your mirror if there are motorcycles loose around so if forced to stop quickly you will be able to leave room for a close following motorcycle to slip by if it cannot stop. Most motorcyclists are optimist "Buppies". They speed crazily in traffic with unbounded fearlessness. They squeeze through traffic at risk of being squashed time and again and come back for more. Watch them . . . like a hawk. It *is* your duty to protect idiots. A dead fool is, very.

## PEDESTRIAN THINKING . . . KEEP IT IN MIND!

Buppy walkers rush to shop before closing time. In downpours they dash for shelter. Fed up waiting, they push prams across the road. Factory bells ring. . .! It's Bingo night—and they're off!

### Blind Walkers

Take trouble to help the blind. If it is safe all round where they wait to cross and you are stopping, a touch on the horn may be used as a signal and you may be able to call through your window.

### Deaf Walkers

You cannot distinguish them so treat everyone on the basis that they might be deaf.

### Old Walkers

Many older people don't understand stopping distances. Usually they are careful but their judgment is faulty. It is simple courtesy to allow plenty of time as their pace is slow; whatever you do, try not to frighten them. There is a special breed, mainly older men, who treat the road as their property. They cross slowly, and smirk as though pleased to trouble you. Perhaps efforts in the last war caused a superiority complex or it's drunkenness but woe betide if you are not aware of this mentality.

## Three Year Old Buppy Children

Nowadays, fortunately, most children have learned to regard traffic seriously by six to nine years old, but the *very young ones still act on whim.*

Fig. 2.   A near miss discussed in the text.

Particularly near suburban schools where parked cars line the streets, DO BE WATCHFUL. Tea times and early morning are worst. *If you killed someone's child, by careless selfish speeding, as simply as swatting a fly dead, your CONSCIENCE would BLEED for life.* Fig. 2 shows an example I witnessed.

A wee girl was standing beside the road *holding her father's hand* as I approached, following behind a delivery van. Concealed from the van driver and myself was her prized doggy. It was still hidden behind the parked car while we were coming along. The kiddy spotted her dog and without warning, wrenched herself free and dashed across towards it. ONLY a superb lightening reaction by the van driver saved her.

The point holds true so often I must ram it home. You cannot assume anything where infants are concerned. THE KIDDIE HOLDING DADDY'S HAND WOULD HAVE FOOLED ninety-nine out of a hundred drivers.

## "THINK WITH" "RUSH-HOUR-ITIS"

Carelessness creeps in if travelling the same route daily. Speeds rise, over-confidence flourishes, rules are broken. Junctions are approached too quickly hoping to whip out smartly. Or the opposite, sleepy, inattentiveness and slowness, relying on knowledge from previous experience.

Non rush-hour examples are bakers' vans, milk floats and child cyclists.

Early birds may even be confronted by one of these "automatic" drivers approaching actually asleep; my advice is hoot strongly, flash headlights and watch his front wheels, and slowing down till he awakes. By watching his wheels, you may be able to swing clear as a last resort.

Allow for all such "rush-hour-itis" is the motto.

## PEAK DANGER PERIODS

Statistics show late Saturday nights to be the most dangerous on the road and worse if wet. This is when the "Buppy" hoards are out in force. Extra care is needed around pub closing times. The message: know the time, think where you are and be prepared. Become a very advanced thinker.

# 2

# *Car Control*

## SLOUCHED BODY—SLOUCHED MIND

Fig. 3 helps explain. *Press* your bottom backward, arch your shoulders well back and you will discover the most relaxed yet *alert* position. The head held high and attentive, you properly command the view near the bonnet that may, in emergency, avoid peril.

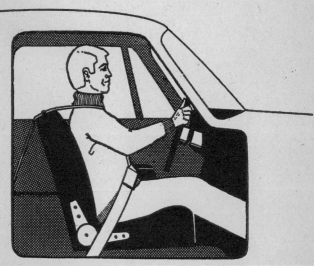

Fig. 3.   Correct way to sit.

### Arms Bent Or Straight?

You need to be able to work the pedals and gears positively, without stretching forward. Your leg should *still be slightly bent when the brake* is pressed hard. (In sports cars, although the legs are more horizontal, the same applies.)

Correct posture aids our sensory system to sound warnings

in the brain. Unless stifled by a sloppy position, balance and listening devices in the ear and nerve messages from all over the body combine to provide essential, integrated information. Steering or braking mechanical faults, changes of road surface, punctures, AND—VITALLY IMPORTANT— THE BEGINNING OF SKIDS—are examples which the sensory detective squad may signal.

You achieve maximum sensitivity, leverage and reaction speed in the arms and hands when the inside elbow angle is 105°–120°. Fully stretched arms are tiring. On the other hand if you steer tucking your elbows close to your chest, you reduce leverage and induce tension. Aim to achieve as near the ideal position described as you can. *Be certain the seat is SECURE after adjustment* or the seat would shoot back and make your brake push ineffective—DEADLY DANGER.

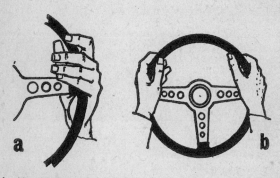

Fig. 4. Hand hold on the wheel.

### Holding The Wheel

Fig. 4 a) shows the sensitive palm area resting on the outside wheel rim. The fingers then wrap round the underside and thumbs point towards 12 o'clock along the top side as in Fig. 4 b). Whether a "nine-fifteen" position is better than one at "ten-to-two" o'clock is doubtful: variation around these positions matters not and is restful but both hands should remain *above the central horizontal spokes*, except for turning.

25

**Many Drivers Never Learned to Steer**

Did you know?

a) Modern "self-centre" steering normally keeps the car straight. Conscious steering creates weaving! Hold the wheel gently, as you would an egg, making the required corrections rather than constant "directions". After small steering movements allow self-centering to operate, lightly controlling the wheel as it returns (no jerks).

On uneven roads the bumps tend to turn the steering. Except on a severe bump, the "self-centering" action of the steering will put the car straight again automatically—if you let it. Hold the steering wheel firmly but allow it to turn slightly and to correct itself as the bumps are encountered. The car will ride straighter than if you "fight" to keep the wheel straight all the time.

b) YOU NEVER CROSS YOUR HANDS. To turn substantially two movements are repeated alternately:

1) The hand next to the turning side *pulls* down while the other loosens grip to slide down and round the wheel so both arrive at the same time near the bottom—ready for movement two.

2) The slipped hand tightens its grip and pushes up, the other relaxing grip sufficiently to glide back ready to repeat (1).

3) You should never turn the wheel of a stationary car. This induces wear; wait till the car is just beginning to move.

**STARTING TIPS**

Starting a car wears the battery. You can prolong battery life by:

a) Switching off electric items—heater, fan, wipers, lights etc. AND

b) Depressing the CLUTCH when starting.

For starting from cold also by:

1. Using brief bursts of starter allowing thirty second rest intervals.

2. For the first burst use CHOKE only, *NO* accelerator, being ready to "catch" it if it starts, with partial accelerator.

3. Second burst as for first.

4. If a third burst is needed use $\frac{3}{4}$ accelerator but push

choke *back off*. Be ready to "catch" this time with the choke, at the same time releasing most of the accelerator. (On certain cars with accelerator pumps avoid agitating the accelerator unnecessarily or neat fuel will be squirted in, flooding the engine).

5. Repeat four.

6. Go back and repeat two, three, four and five in order. When all this fails check:

a) Ignition is switched on.

b) Anti-theft device.

c) Petrol. (Note: gauge may be faulty.)

d) Battery terminals for tightness.

e) The firm, DRY, attachment of plug leads to distributor and all leads to coil.

The mechanically minded might then clean and adjust contact breaker and plug gaps.

BUT if the battery sounds weak try the handle or a push or tow. 3rd gear is usually best for a push or tow start. (2nd in three gear cars.) Remember ignition and choke! Automatic transmission cars can be push/tow started if the selector is moved to L *from N* at about 20 m.p.h., as a rule, *but follow the instruction book of your own model.*

**Choke Tips**

A finger held on the choke knob while in use prevents forgetting to put it back. The "fast" tickover is your double safety reminder, if you have left choke on.

**HANDBRAKE TIPS**

Apart from "fly-off" handbrakes, avoid the click, click, click of the ratchet by using the ratchet release; it saves wear.

Outside my office where there is a "pull in" for cigarettes etc., parked cars regularly "run away". Because the ground looks flat, any half hearted grab at the handbrake seems to do for many people in a rush. They do not think of leaving a gear engaged (or selecting P—automatic) to give the double safety of engine compression hold. It is astonishing how often this REALLY DOES HAPPEN through slovenly habits of drivers involved.

Fig. 5 shows extra safe hill parking with the front wheels "chocked", almost touching the kerb, but not pressing on it (to avoid tyre damage). You mustn't bang the wheel against the

The front wheels are 'chocked' almost touching the kerb.

Fig. 5. Hill parking.

kerb during parking, or steering and tyre damage may result. If you park facing up a hill which has *no kerb* to "chock" against leave the steering turned so that should the car move the back will run *into* the edge, not *out*. Always lock the doors to safeguard against the risk of theft or inquisitive children who might tamper with the brake.

## USING THE CLUTCH

Pressing the clutch fully downward is unnecessary; just beyond the "biting point" suffices. You can establish the minimum necessary amount to depress it with practice.

Should there be no room to rest your foot left of the clutch pedal, raise your knee so your foot rests flat in front of the pedal. Don't drive touching the clutch pedal or you may wear the clutch.

## GEARS THAT WON'T GO IN
### She Won't Go Into First

Try a) Clutch up fully, rest a few seconds, then right down try again. b) Second trick: clutch down, engine ticking over— gently ease in the lever as you gradually raise the pedal. At some point she'll go. c) Trick three: except uphill, move off in second gear. d) On an uphill you can release the handbrake enough to slip the car $\frac{1}{2}''$ back. Trick a) above usually now works.

On the move, unless the clutch or gears are damaged or broken fourth or top gear will always engage. If she won't change from first to second, skip into third. When second to third is the problem, take top. Trouble changing down the gears is usually overcome by *braking* to slow the car and releasing the clutch once, momentarily, in neutral, then "in".

Never force gears in, (lever may be hitting edge of slot). Fingerlight, directionally precise, pressure guides the lever to its groove.

### To Avoid Grating Into First Gear

A non-syncromesh 1st gear may grate when engaging it at rest. You are trying to align a still cog to one which is spinning. But the revolving of the spinning cog gradually peters out once you have put the clutch down. If you wait a second for this cog to stop, 1st should engage silently. It helps the cog to stop if the engine only ticks over.

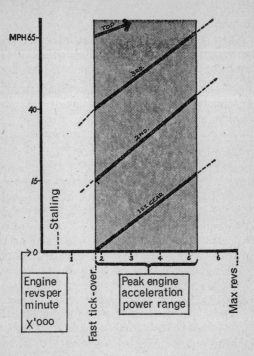

Fig. 6.   Peak engine power.

## SAVE FUEL AND ... ACCELERATE!
Top ECONOMICAL performance can be with the acceleration pedal only three quarters down! Even when accelerating briskly you improve speed little by using the last quarter. Nor does "flat out" driving need the foot on the floor, while at medium speed you may slack off the pedal a surprising amount without losing speed.

### Are you in the Right Gear, Dear?
Fig. 6 graphs peak engine acceleration power for an average saloon. Fastest, cheapest acceleration keeps inside the power

range in all gears. A speed outside this range in any gear wastes fuel and *loses time*.

## Restful Cruising

On some cars you can help your foot maintain cruising speed against the spring loaded action of the accelerator by lodging your accelerator shoe against the side of the floor-well. Friction holds it steady, but be sure your foot won't get stuck!

## THE UPHILL START JOKE

Even fairly advanced motorists may benefit from the following explanation. Few seem to understand that *provided engine revs are held sufficiently high to move the car forward up the hill, there is one point of release at which the clutch pedal can be HELD which stops the car rolling back downhill* (*handbrake off*), but at which the gear is insufficiently engaged, (because the clutch is not fully released), to move the car uphill. You are suspended between going up and rolling back. To start expertly uphill you bring the clutch to this "biting point" and maintain it; then let the handbrake off calmly and slightly add acceleration as you steadily release the remaining clutch.

Save time at slightly uphill brief stops by holding her on the footbrake. To go, take first, bring the clutch to just before the "biting point", steady it and quickly switch the right foot to the accelerator to speed up the engine. Adjust that clutch a fraction up (if necessary) and there you are, *suspended between going and rolling back* as if you had used the handbrake.

## FOOTBRAKE TECHNIQUE

Braking effort comes more from the thigh than the ankle muscles.

To smooth out braking adjust your push from the thigh. If you brake slightly more than necessary to begin with this enables you to ease off and allows a jerk free "roll stop". Earlier and therefore safer warning of brake failure or a skiddy surface is a safety bonus of this technique. You sense the retarding effect through your hands, by balance in the ear and by the amount of strength you use in your arms and legs to counteract being thrown forward.

# DOUBLE DE-CLUTCHING

This has a twofold purpose: 1) To help the gear cogs engage; 2) To pre-adjust the engine speed so that it matches the transmission speed required by the new gear for the same speed of the car—just before the clutch is released.

The better the matching of the speeds in 2) the less jerk will be felt by passengers as the new gear becomes engaged.

With modern syncromesh gearboxes the need for 1) above has diminished. For this reason a half way stage towards a double de-clutch has become a popular technique and I describe it first. It is only necessary for downward changes.

1) Depress clutch at the same time releasing the accelerator (left foot down—right foot up).

2) Select next gear down without delay.

3) "Blip" the accelerator quickly. Release the clutch, timing the moment the gear will "bite" into engagement to coincide with the peak revs of your blip on the accelerator, or well before they have died away. Just how big a "blip" to give for a particular speed and when precisely to release the clutch comes with practice. The principle of the full double de-clutch advocated by the "old school" is as follows: The principle of matching the engine speed is the same.

*The movements are carried out as quickly in succession as possible:*

1) Clutch down—release accelerator, at the same time.

2) Slip gear to neutral.

3) Release clutch, fully.

4) "Blip" accelerator.

5) Clutch down fast, select next gear down, release clutch at once—while the extra engine revs last.

With a minimum of practice all these moves can be completed at lightning speed, although it looks a long job on paper.

The need to double de-clutch when changing *up* the gears is almost extinct but may apply to a few historic cars. The method is 1) as above, 2) and 3) as above, *leave out* 4) and 5) you simply engage the next gear up and release the clutch—then re-accelerate as you would after a normal gear change (if required). The moves are the same except you *do without the accelerator "blip"*.

## HEEL AND TOE GEAR CHANGING

This technique could equally be called heel and toe braking. Its purpose is to enable you to drop down the gears *during* braking so that when the need for slowing is passed you are already geared for maximum re-acceleration. The lower gears also help the brakes and give a more controlled stop. If you have mastered the double de-clutch or have perfected the half way stage to the DDC which was described first, you can combine either method with the heel and toe principle.

Fig. 7 shows how the heel of your shoe, or just the right side

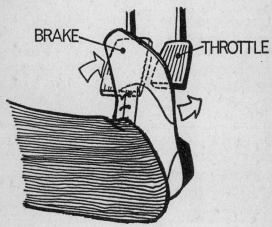

Fig. 7. Heel and toe.

of the sole can be used to blip the accelerator pedal while the ball of the foot still keeps continuous breaking pressure. This feels strange to begin with but with practice it becomes possible to maintain any level of braking pressure evenly, despite blipping the accelerator as much as you wish! If trying this for the first time choose moments when there is no traffic around you. And when you haven't *got* to stop!

## SWITCHING OFF YOUR INDICATORS "AUTOMATICALLY"

To ensure your indicator is *never* left on, make a habit to lightly touch the control arm with one finger as you straighten the steering wheel after your turn. This is sufficient on most cars to make the spring loaded control flick to its "off" position. When you indicate for slight turns, a finger held on the control reminds you.

# 3

# *Town Technique*

## MAIN ROADS IN THE TOWN

*In large cities the important "through" roads and "ring" routes mostly have at least two lanes each way. Sometimes opposing traffic is separated only by bollards placed at regular intervals; sometimes there are stretches of fully equipped duel carriageway. Single line two-way conditions are encountered from time to time where there hasn't been room to build the road wider or subsequently widen it. I shall first discuss driving on these roads which usually carry most of the traffic.*

In driving, if a general philosophy can be established and its principles adhered to, a lot of difficulties can be removed or solved. Reading this book will, I hope, help develop a sound driving philosophy for you as you absorb, reject or improve the principles explained about many aspects of driving. Here is one general principle I have found useful.

## KEEPING TO THE RIGHT HAND LANE WHEN THERE IS MORE THAN ONE

Normally where there are two or more lanes each way the right one is quicker and safer to use, regardless of speed limits, because of three facts. 1) You have a reduced accident risk from side turnings and openings and from pedestrians or children stepping off the pavement. 2) You have no problems with parked cars. Inner lane vehicles often have to pull out to pass parked cars and by custom find they first have to give way to any vehicles overtaking themselves. The fear that some idiot may open his car door in your path is also removed. 3) You join the ranks of other, thinking, advanced right lane professionals, by-passing and keeping out of the way of those of the inner lane dawdling mentality. On average you have an easier ride in the right hand lane.

It's not all sunshine in the right hand lane however. People

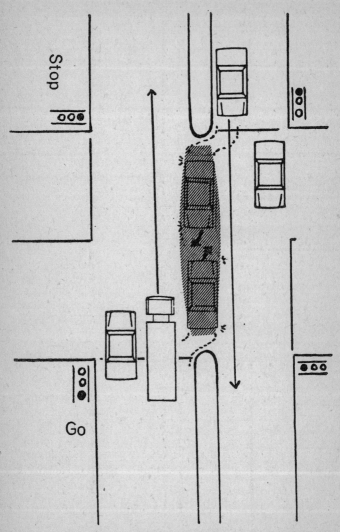

Fig. 8 (a). Keeping out of people's way when turning at lights.

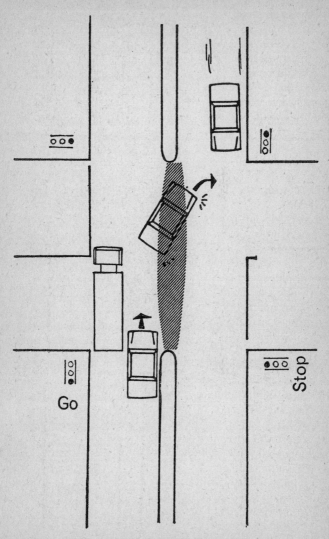

Fig. 8 (b).   Baulking "straight ahead" traffic by bad positioning

ahead waiting to turn right can baulk you and then you must be adaptable. Good long range anticipation should give you plenty time to move discreetly to the inner lane. A car which fails to signal till too late ought not to fool you because you will have seen his vagueness in positioning and his speed reduction and you should be ready to act whatever he does.

Sometimes, for example at lights, one or even two cars, positioned correctly in readiness to make a right turn when the oncoming traffic clears, need not baulk straight-on traffic at all. Fig. 8 (a) shows how a good driver can cocoon himself in safety in the shaded area provided he gets his car parallel to the road once he has driven in there. He as it were "manufactures" room for people originally behind him to flow through straight on. Fig. 8 (b) shows how a buppy blocks everyone.

In a particular instance therefore, if only one person ahead signals right, or perhaps two at a very large intersection, you may be able to pre-judge whether you are going to be left room to go through straight on or will have to change lane. A part of your judgement will be the opinion you have reached during following as to the quality of the driver in question!

There is bound to be the odd time however when changing to the inside lane before it is too late proves impossible without risking ill feeling or danger. A professional never forces his way across or cuts in; rather does he ease imperceptably over when there is a "long" gap. It causes no harm to a driver if you occupy a sensible gap ahead of him when you are travelling at his speed. What is unfair is to squeeze in so that he has to slow up. You must be patient for a fair gap. In law too, you must wait.

Suppose you have moved to or were in the inner lane because of someone turning right. There is an easy way to regain the right hand lane at once. Move back to the outer lane as you pass him as illustrated by Fig. 9. It is almost certain nothing could be overtaking you at this stage so it is a safe manoeuvre from that viewpoint but look out for motor cycles trying to sneak past *either* side of you. Also be on guard for traffic from the other direction turning across you out of the area shaded in Fig. 9. They may be concealed from you till the last second by the vehicle you are getting round.

Now I have outlined the mental approach to right lane

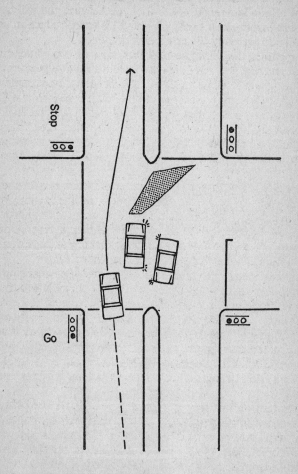

Fig. 9.   Regaining the right hand lane.

driving here is a tip with which you can help drivers behind who have a similar philosophy.

## HELPING LANE DECISIONS FOR FOLLOWERS

The lights turn red and you are the first person to stop in the right hand lane. No one was immediately behind you but the stream on the inner lane has already formed quite a long queue. Perhaps a minute ticks by and you notice in the far range in your mirror a car coming cautiously in the outside lane. He is clearly uncertain whether you might be going to turn right and is already nudging his way over towards the inside lane. A straight on signal, as you would give a policeman, which he can see silhouetted through your rear window, is just the message he's praying for! See Fig. 10.

When you wish to turn right yourself, please be considerate to the right lanesters who are behind! If you are going to be the front man waiting to turn, signal very early and maintain it if stopped, at least till several are behind you and winking. This gives those a long way behind a chance to anticipate the blockage accurately and in time. Should you cancel your indicator

Fig. 10. Silhouetted signal for drivers behind.

while waiting (sometimes a relief for people's eyes at night or in rain) hold your finger on the control arm to remind you to reapply it before going.

A final word on the right lane philosophy: one has no right to cling to the right lane if anyone wishes to pass. As soon as safely possible, move to the inner lane to let them through. Now, another principle which can help you a lot.

## TACTICS FOR KEEPING A CLEAR SPACE AHEAD OF YOU—ANOTHER DRIVING PHILOSOPHY

The professional likes the road immediately ahead uncluttered by Buppies. (Buppies were explained in chapter 1). Having a clear stretch in front is a safer proposition than jogging along in the middle or at the back of a stream. You can see the problems that lie ahead to the fullest advantage. You have room to manoeuvre.

To this end whenever there is an opportunity to move ahead of an immediate stream an advanced driver will take it. Once there he will not immediately race on to the back of the next block of traffic, but will bide his time, without holding up those he has just passed, so that he retains his clear space ahead advantage for as long as reasonably possible.

Similarly if a chance occurs to allow a bunch of traffic in front to get away, this is another way to ensure a clear space ahead for a while.

Fig. 11. Choosing the empty lane.

The right hand lane principle keeps you moving past many bunches of traffic. Here are a few more hints. You are

41

approaching a red traffic light as the artist shows in Fig. 11. If you choose the one free lane early and use careful timing so that you arrive in the front row as green appears you may often overtake the whole "bunch" safely. But you must beware of pedestrians straying across and maniacs shooting red crossing your bows.

When you are waiting in a front line position at lights there may be the opportunity to get clear of bunching vehicles, especially if you are in the right lane. Over enthusiasm for a "Grand Prix" start however, *invites death*. And racing is illegal. Nevertheless a swift getaway is usually advantageous but do remember the following: motor cycles may have squeezed close either side—bollards or the pavement line ahead may be going to force you off course—and the light shooting deamons operate more in fog, snow and on wet nights! *Flashing your eyes* continuously to spot them in time is essential.

In getting off the mark quickly bear in mind the best power range of your engine, shown by Fig. 6, and that snappy gear changes save seconds. A sloppy change loses valuable yards. Changing too early, or too late, will lose you ground.

\* \* \*

Some notes to remember along with these two principles I have outlined—right laning and keeping a clear space ahead—are these. If you mistakenly select a green filter lane which says go, GO! and go the way the arrow points. Accept your misfortune as a punishment—you have no right to baulk correctly positioned drivers.

The Highway Code cautions you . . . "in a traffic hold up, do not try to jump the queue by cutting into another lane, or by overtaking the vehicles in front of you". The wise driver therefore makes use of any spare lane or space which would otherwise be wasted but without cutting in, without taking any "unfair" advantage and never in a way which might hinder others.

While much of the Code is not law, in practice much of the law supports it! But the expert can often, without discourtesy, get far ahead of the inexperienced, and his doing so leaves more room for the novice—a bonus frequently overlooked.

**Changing Lane When a Chance Presents Itself—Rather Than When You Want To—Can Save Time For All**

Imagine as an example, middle laning *in thick traffic* on a *three* lane dual carriageway, knowing that you will need to turn right before long. The turn you require need not yet be in sight when it happens that someone alongside or just behind in the outside lane starts to signal left. This is your chance to signal right, watch his reaction and, all being well, you will be able to scissor-swap gaps. Neither of you need slow more than a fraction. It may be a driver ahead who is indicating left and searching his mirror who provides your opportunity. Acting when opportunity knocks, instead of at the last second before the turn, saves a hold up for *both* lanes!

## THE IMPORTANCE OF EYE RANGING

Eye ranging near and far ahead, each side, and mirror-wise close and far behind, *all the time*, is a tonic for eye muscles and is the key to knowing the changing requirements around you. An all-round running picture, as it were, needs to be constantly focussing in your mind—a finer computer than which was never made.

### Bringing Science to Sight

Hawk-eyed vision is developed rather than inborn and is methodical. As the scene continually unfolds in front of him the expert plans so that he can always be looking in the right direction at the right time. In order to be able to concentrate on the supreme potentially dangerous points as they are reached every opportunity of seeing behind trees, obstacles, parked vans—and *under* these as well—through railings, round beyond and underneath as well as *through* a car in front and so on, has to be taken as it arises. An opportunity not taken at once is usually lost once you get closer. The chance must be seized while it is there.

The opportunist who grabs his chances for glances thereby leaves more time for decisions and for focussing repeatedly on the extra risk areas he has pin-pointed well in advance. Openings from lanes and wandering children are examples.

The experienced, healthy, exercised eye continually casts everywhere, letting the brain decide whether each problem can be passed without slowing. Areas in between risky points are not dismissed. These are taken in and assessed during safer moments and this way no time is lost. Everything is covered. There may well be only one safe moment when a particularly difficult hazard can be checked. The expert will aim to check it at that moment.

The scope for vision may often be increased by re-positioning your car slightly to one side or the other. All round running knowledge must confirm first that this is safe and you must avoid abrupt weaving, and no zig-zagging! Adjustment of the gap ahead between you and the next car can be another visual aid. It is a continuing process of using wits to see "everything" everywhere.

On nearing a danger point and assessing it, accident risk is increasing rapidly. Speed must be controlled as necessary and *disciplined*. Position may need to be altered to your safety advantage, above all being sure you have space into which to swerve and stop safely. Be ready for any happening is my motto—including the most extraordinary.

### Preparatory Moves That Make "Danger" Safe

Nearing possible trouble, a finger rests at the horn ready for a toot which could prevent a crisis, the feet *hover* over brake and clutch to reduce stopping distance. Speed, in check anyway, is restricted to occasional dabs of acceleration at safer moments but the brake foot needs to be ever ready to bring you to a sudden stop if the possible emergency happens. The mind must anticipate. Spaces for escape by swerving are constantly reviewed and taken into account.

In the desperate unpredictability of an unforeseeable emergency, "running knowledge"—almost without conscious thought—is essential if alternatives to disaster are to be found.

It is not enough to keep your eyes roving. The gaze must never dwell but should range widely, repeatedly. Circumstances change like lightning as the child breaking from the father's grasp illustrated a few pages back. Be alert.

Accident victims are often uncertain *what happened*, so perhaps I may be forgiven for reiterating the importance of constant attention and thought while driving, till it becomes instinctive with experience.

Eye muscle tiredness can be avoided if you sometimes let

the neck flex freely. Neck exercise also reduces the risk of becoming an old stiff-necked accident-prone motorist!

## AND NOW THE MIRRORS
CORRECT USE OF THE MIRROR IS THE SECRET WHICH ENABLES POSITIONING SO THAT TRAFFIC BEHIND ALWAYS HAS PLENTY OF ADVANCE WARNING OF YOUR INTENTIONS. By having this advance knowledge following drivers are deterred from trying to pass you when you will soon be turning or changing lanes. It is also the key to foreknowledge in emergency. 95% concentration must be towards the front so perhaps 5% is mirror time.

Use skill, glancing in the mirror while the road is safe ahead so that the mirror is not a distraction if danger arises.

It is sometimes vital, before deciding if you dare re-position or what-ever, to confirm the proximity of what is behind or to the side, by a rapid over-shoulder glance during a safe moment. Many "L" teachers discourage this. The result is thousands of

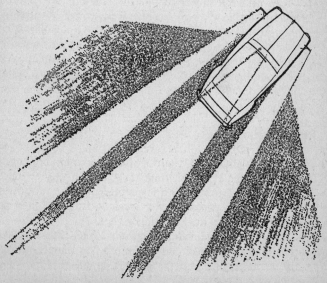

Fig. 12.   Mirror blind spots.

inflexible drivers who never take to an essential safety technique. Develop it from now onwards.

You need enough mirror use to picture all that is behind and what is behind that and vaguely further behind. No need to know the shape of the girl driver, only of her existence, whether she is closing, falling back or holding her position. *ONLY frequent glances enable you to pick out cars and motor cycles, which can be masked or missed by occasional mirror-use. (See blind spots shown in* Fig. 12.) But mirror vision is obtained by quick glances, no more, as the eyes' main task is watching the front and sides.

### Are Mirrors Enough At Traffic Lights?

No. Cars and cycles creep up while you wait. A look round before moving registers in your mind their existence and position—ESSENTIAL INFORMATION If You Are Turning.

### Mirror Art

Imagine a lorry thundering close behind and you are preparing to overtake a slower car ahead. You can only see the lorry radiator badge in the mirror. How can you check nothing is zipping past both of you before you start to move out? The answer is to slow gradually a little, then accelerate to create a gap between you and the lorry enabling you to obtain the mirror coverage needed. Or, if the road bends, even a little, you may find the vision needed in the mirror. A wing-mirror can help.

### Mirror Courtesy

The mirror informs you of overtakers, and followers preparing to turn right or left. Courtesy demands your help where possible and safe. You sometimes benefit many behind you whereas thoughtlessness, even for a second, can create a hold up.

Fig. 13 shows a thoughtless driver who blocks the road instead of keeping parallel and in the shaded area. Bare inches over and everyone behind could have moved on, and this would also have opened the junction further back for the crossing traffic. One road-clog can cause a mile of trouble! A short polite hoot sometimes "instructs" such an erring driver if he still has room to correct his mistake. It is so selfish and happens so often.

Moving in for overtakers, even only a little, *confirms you know they are passing* and is almost as vital as promoting their safe pass. Unfortunately trained mirror users, except at turns, are almost non-existent in Britain, especially among our appalling "week-end" drivers.

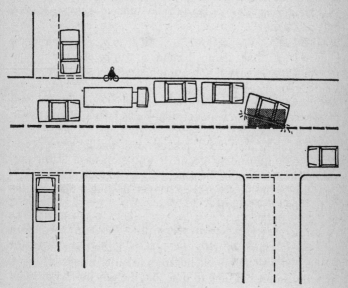

Fig. 13. A thoughtless driver or road-clog.

## Lapse of Mirrors—"Running"—Knowledge

Even a good mirror user occasionally forgets and lands in trouble without knowing whether swerving might swipe a scooterist to his death. To swing to avert one disaster can create another. Swerving into an unseen passing car may push it through a wall.

Except in desperation (e.g. a child running out or a head-on crash which *must* be avoided). *STOP* or slow down unless you know you can swerve safely.

You will often find there *is* stopping time anyway. Fools who swerve first are likely to pay later!

47

A second principle for mirror defaulters which helps to prevent being smashed into from behind, (the accident which may cause "whip-lash" i.e. breaks your neck) is this: IN EMERGENCY, BRAKE ONLY AS HARD AS SPACE DICTATES YOU HAVE TO.

Once sure you can stop, adjust braking to use all the space you have, *so giving the chap behind a chance*.

### Conscious avoidance of the Killer "Whiplash" Smash from Behind

Brake lights warn followers . . . if they work! Your brake lights reflect on headlamps behind, so can be checked in your mirror while queuing if you are too lazy to check them with a friend!

Flash them to alert followers *in advance* of probable stopping by lightly touching the brake pedal—a technique of great value especially at speed, if you see possible danger far ahead!

Emergencies apart, to stop suddenly is madness, yet people do it. Idiotic offenders are those who stop on a "clearway" about three feet out in the road, perhaps to look at their map! As they are too far from the kerb fast flowing traffic may not realise they have stopped.

### BRAKING AND TRAFFIC FLOW

Imagine two lanes of traffic going in each direction on a busy urban clearway. Traffic lights, pedestrian crossings etc. force traffic to stop from time to time, but the general forward flow is swift.

You can plan *your* driving to help keep this flow going if you follow a few simple rules. The more people who do so the smoother the flow will be.

1) After any stop, add speed swiftly, till you regain the flow speed.
2) In the same way, just as you should avoid the dawdle start, avoid the dawdle stop. No sudden stopping, which risks the rear-end pile-up both for you and others further behind.

   Judge your stops so that your brake application has to be at about 25% of foot pressure when compared with the force you apply for an emergency stop. Slowing more gradually is a good fault but the trouble is—from a traffic flow point of view—that the drivers behind you will tend to see your early brake lights as a loud warning. In turn they will slow *more* than you have. Not so very far behind you the line of cars can come to a stop while you are still moving, albeit slowly!

Then, because so few are nifty picking up speed again, the flow is broken for the cars involved. You may not have had to stop before the reason for stopping removed itself but they will find themselves stopped after it has gone!

Had you left your braking till later; a) the reason for stopping could have cleared itself before you needed to brake. Traffic could then have continued uninterrupted; b) if a stop was still necessary, the whole line would have to stop anyway so no-one would lose.

3) Moving traffic frequently has to slow a little, perhaps while someone turns off, and then it picks up speed and flows on. Rather like stopping too gradually, if *you* slow more or earlier than necessary, drivers behind will too. And in turn the effect will be magnified as the reaction spreads along the line behind. So braking for slowing should also be judged, leaving it till application at about 25% of foot pressure is needed.

**Reveal Indicators Ahead to Others Behind**

Once someone ahead indicates, and if "running" knowledge shows it is safe, re-position to enable the driver behind to see the signal. You move slightly right or left as required. This is quicker than a hand signal which may even disguise the prob-

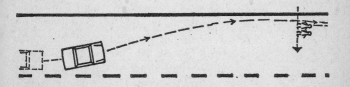

Fig. 14. The "steering" message.

lem and fool traffic behind into stopping, instead of preparing to filter.

Your sideways movement also confirms to the driver ahead, via his mirror, that you have *accepted* his signal.

If he is overtaking traffic ahead, rather than turning, your movement confirms that you understand and will not begin to pass as he pulls out.

### Re-positioning Calms Pedestrians

You may be going fast on a wide road when pedestrians start to cross too close for comfort. Rule 1 is ease your foot on the accelerator and brake if necessary. But, *where safe, give pedestrians the "steering" message*. Then they know at once you will take care of them. The driver in Fig. 14 tells the walkers he has seen them by pointing his car temporarily behind them as well as braking. In different circumstances "steering" messages by you can be given to help other motorists. The art should be developed.

## NOSE-TO-TAIL

Fig. 15 shows a wide traffic light junction clogged with traffic, of which that turning left is at the most doing 12 to 15 m.p.h. A dangerous speed nevertheless.

Car A (Fig. 15) nose-to-tail behind one lorry has been hurried by amber appearing; the other lorry prevents moving to the inner lane. All three are turning left and keeping lane discipline but the right hand lorry masks an oncoming scooterist from Car A.

### Nose to Tail "Grass Roots" Principle

The danger in this example is common to many situations and a cautious grass-roots principle can often save life.

Keep your whole car—including the right hand front corner of the bonnet—tucked within the space just used by the larger vehicle ahead. If you allow that corner of the bonnet even a fraction over that line, as car A *has* in Fig. 15, you risk a crash with such a scooter. The rear right hand corner of the lorry prevents you seeing him till it is too late. I have put a star where the scooterist could collide with your wing.

The lorry must now be allowed to pull away well ahead before you ease out to see beyond it.

50

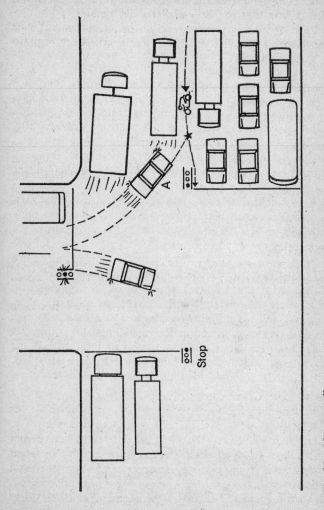

A

Stop

Fig. 15. Nose-to-tail.

## TURNING-OFF PRINCIPLE

Part 1—Get off the main road quickly! (Where safe.)

Part 2—Where you can, position to permit following through
traffic to flow on; use every inch of available safe
space!

Turning quickly applies more to left turns than right,
though if several are behind you ready to turn right, your
quickness may provide opportunity for an extra car or two to
follow safely. Except where the opening is blind or pedestrians
prevent you, be snappy is the motto for left turns. Dawdling
frustrates the stream following and may force them to brake,
go down the gears, or even jam on—probably unnecessarily.
Using space to the last inch must include "slip-offs"—from
where they start! Many roads and modernised "through"
routes are now designed so that a turning car can slip off the
main carriageway up to 30 or 50 yards before the turn. The
pavement is deliberately set back. But the majority of motorists
do not make use of them. However a polite toot sometimes
encourages people. An equally usable "slip on" is normal for
those coming out of such turnings.

### For Turning Left An "Unofficial" Signal May Be Easier

If the road is otherwise clear it may be safe for a waiting car
to pull out as you turn in. Your "steering" message by correct
positioning and speed reduction confirms your indicator but a
hand signal removes all doubt. The official signal is correct but
Fig. 16 shows an "unofficial" one, easier to give (especially in
wet weather), which shows through modern cars with wide
(unobstructed) windows. In different circumstances this extra

Fig. 16.   Unofficial left signal for those behind.

signal confirms to those behind that you *will* be turning. Few people trust indicators alone!

## Make Time While Green Lasts

Imagine you are going to turn right at some traffic lights a little way ahead and that they are showing green. The road *you will enter* has two lanes on your side. Approaching the lights from the opposite direction there is only one car and its driver makes a definite signal that he is going to turn left, into the same road as you are going to enter.

If you are extremely careful you may be able to save seconds by entering the road side by side, you into the outer lane, and he into the left hand one. What you do is to encourage him to turn neatly into the inner line by nosing craftily forward as he approaches the turn. *But don't commit yourself* until you can see that he will co-operate. Any crash might be judged as your fault.

## MAKING VISUAL SAFETY WHEN YOU HELPFULLY STOP FOR PEOPLE

Fig. 1, page 20, shows stopping well back to ease the task for a lorry driver coming out who, due to his length, has to "cut" the corner. On a "through" route where drivers in two lanes have to stop, the "well back" principle is doubly important. What is also vital is the wide angle of vision the lorry driver, or any driver needs in order to see if any motor-cycle is passing *you*. You prevent accidents by giving such a turning driver the chance to see for himself if it is safe.

## JOINING "THROUGH" ROUTES FROM SIDE ROADS AT "T" JUNCTIONS

Traffic sweeping along in double streams need not be so hard to join.

### Turning Left, Joining a Road with Two Lanes Each Way

By taking a good forward position you are ready if it is safe to cut time by tucking into a gap in the left lane without waiting for right lanesters to clear. Even if you require to cross to the outer lane almost at once (so as to leave the road to the right) the task may become easier if you can use the left lane first as you would an acceleration lane.

53

As soon as you are in the left hand lane, signal for moving to the right lane. Watching in your mirror and over the shoulder if need be, get over at the first safe gap which will leave the drivers now behind you time to note you will soon turn right.

### "Forget-Me-Not!" Cries The Mirror at Every Junction

*Even in the seconds of turning* (right or left) cars can arrive behind which were not in sight when you last looked. It happens frequently on fast routes but you can also be surprised on less busy roads.

*Develop a Saving System: Make a Habit invariably to check the mirror* as you straighten up. You thus come to associate straightening up with the mirror checking, and will always do it. You are automatically alerted if it is necessary to accelerate swiftly away from any arriving speedster, or should you need to make room immediately for one to pass.

### Turning Right, Joining a Road With Two Lanes Each Way

Increasing traffic has created a situation at some "T" junctions where unless you tackle them in two halves, blocking traffic from the right first, you may wait even for hours.

Crawling traffic is sometimes safely persuaded to stop if you edge out cautiously. You dare not shoot out and risk an accident with fast traffic from your right. If however this has ceased for a long space and there is nothing turning right from the other direction into your road, this is your cue to move out and block the two lanes on your side. Great care is needed. You must be sure anyone coming from the right can see you for a long distance.

Despite occasional ill-mannered hooting as drivers have to pull up, they have no greater right to the main road than you have to wait on it prior to going right. That is, so long as you got there first when the road was clear.

Enormous care in selecting where this can be safely done is required. At night, for example, it can be highly dangerous as you may not be seen. Usually risk of being hit while waiting can be reduced by stopping at an angle thus not completely blocking your side of the road.

You now turn right as soon as you can, applying similar techniques to those explained above for "Turning Left, Joining a Road with Two Lanes Each Way".

While waiting, if any car from your left begins to signal for turning right to where you came from, as he is slowing up and positioning there may be time for you to accelerate briskly into the outer lane he will vacate. (Traffic behind him will be filtering to his left or blocked).

Watch out for zebra crossings or anything that could prevent you reaching your new stream speed quickly because traffic now behind you, concentrating on your manoeuvre, may fail to notice that you must stop.

## Crossing "Through" routes

Similarly, blocking traffic on your right may be the one hope here. Then traffic from the left, seeing your situation, often stops and lets you over.

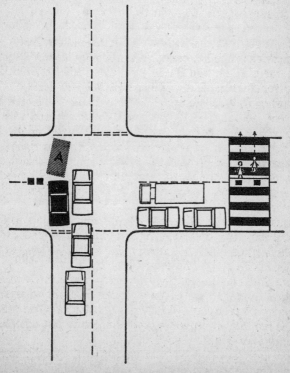

Fig. 17. "Doubling" (see text).

Once *all* the main road traffic *has stopped*, it is sensible for *all* the crossing traffic to be allowed over. Otherwise time is only lost for another bunch of main road traffic which will have to pull up.

If you are tailing across while a gap is available you should keep close but being wary as main road traffic creeps forward. *Look out either way for mopeds queue jumping blindly in these situations.*

If there is "solid" traffic the advanced driver occasionally helps the progress of the crossing traffic by resorting to "doubling" as shown in Fig. 17. Much depends on the width of the opening into the main road.

Normally at junctions of this kind drivers wishing to go straight ahead wait near the centre line, leaving room for anyone going left to filter out. In "rush hour" conditions it is fast becoming customary for expert drivers to form a second straight on queue in this space. Then, as each driver in the normal queue edges out to block traffic from his right, the leading driver in the "second queue" moves out beside him—making use of the protection from traffic from the right that his blocking movement affords. The position recorded by Fig. 17 shows an expert in this "protected" position. He and the other front driver moved out to block the first half of the road while the lorry and stopped cars from the right were waiting the other side of the zebra as the walkers crossed.

The "expert" may now need to take the initiative in blocking traffic coming from the left when the first safe opportunity occurs BUT, according to the width of road available, he must be prepared to wait in the shadowed position A, in Fig. 17, if by trying to go first he might squeeze the "normal" driver too far over on to the offside of the road being entered.

### "Doubling" When Turning Right Onto A Road With Two Lanes Each Way

A similar technique has become recognised as more efficient at many T-joins. Some have arrows on the road to confirm this. The method can be cautiously employed.

The "doubling" driver, having eased out while protected from the right by a driver beside him in the normal queue, then moves forward to block traffic from the left at the first safe opportunity. (This may be possible immediately if no traffic

56

comes from the left). If the driver in the normal queue now makes his turn neatly into the outside lane there should be plenty of room for the "doubling" driver to make the turn side by side with him, into the inside lane. But the "doubling" driver must be prepared to wait in the blocking position if there is not enough space, to give precedence to the normal queue driver (and any who tail efficiently behind him) to get away first. While waiting beforehand the "doubling" car should keep a few feet back so as not to block the first car's view left. You ought not to use this technique if by waiting in the "doubling" position you will be blocking traffic behind you which wishes to turn left. Only use it where the width is such that you are still leaving them room to get away left.

## ZEBRA CROSSING SAFETY

Your brake lights warn followers as you stop. Watch that any driver alongside you *is* also stopping. An arm stopping signal at zebras is good and tells the pedestrians you will be stopping. The danger is that approaching drivers from the other direction may not see it. An advanced answer gaining favour is two prolonged headlight flashes which are sure to alert a dreamy driver.

## HEADLIGHT FLASHING

The Highway Code discourages headlight flashing other than in situations where you would hoot. The code is not the law or the beginning or end of road wisdom. Before describing certain customary uses of headlight flashing, let us consider the use as an alternative to the horn.

1. If a driver hugs the centre of the road and you want to pass you can often alert him from his sleep-driving, without noisy hooting, by a flash or two. Especially at night or in dull weather this catches his eyes in his mirror or screen and he moves to the left.

2. At night, at crossings, passing etc. un-dipping and dipping form a silent substitute to the horn and used within reason are excellent safety aids. They are often more effective than the horn.

3. While passing in daytime, some drivers flash once only but if side roads exist this can be confusing. In busy parts, especially the "killer" 3 lane two way road, to keep headlights

*on all the time* while passing does indicate to others "I am coming through".

### Headlight Flashing Customs

Despite the Code a customary and courteous use of headlight flashing has developed and is increasing, I think wisely. You use them at your own risk. In theory the Code may be right but in practice flashing exists and we have to live in the traffic world around us.

1. To confirm to someone waiting in a side road to your left that *you are* pulling up to allow him to join the main road in front of you. You *only* flash while you are stopped or almost.

2. Similarly to confirm that you wish a driver from the opposite direction waiting positioned to turn right, to cross in front of you.

3. Where you are waiting to turn right off a main road through nose-to-tail traffic, (which will lose nothing by waiting while you turn), you can often induce courtesy by switching on your lights. The usual reply saying, "Yes, in front of me" is a short return flash. Traffic clogged behind you is freed from a senseless hold-up as a bonus.

4. In faster traffic, when in the same waiting position, having headlamps on may alert the fastard who overtakes towards you, apparently unaware you are stopped!

5. When towing, driving a long or wide cargo etc. use day-time headlights. Police, fire engines and ambulances often use daytime headlights.

6. Constant on-off flashing is used to warn oncomers that there has been an accident behind you.

Unfortunately, flashes as in 1 or 2 above are occasionally used by ignorant drivers, or drivers adhering to the "letter" of the Highway Code to mean the opposite, i.e. "You stop—I'm coming through". *You must, therefore, never trust such signals unless confirmed by the driver concerned slowing down: you must also be sure no-one is passing him.*

Before flashing the giver has the duty to think on behalf of everyone who will see the flash to ensure none might mis-interpret it.

Beware of your "come-on" flash to a distant motorist which could invite someone nearer and unexpected by you or UNEXPECTED BY SOMEONE ELSE.

Some people flash to warn you of a radar police trap but this is illegal.

## TRAFFIC LIGHT KNOWLEDGE

When loaded vehicles head the queue at lights they are slow away and rarely mind smaller fry using narrow spaces to squeeze to the front ready to go at green. To be safe, cautiously edge your bonnet slightly ahead so that the heavy vehicle driver sees you (especially if on his nearside). You will also see last minute pedestrians. Even with ample room this advanced technique can be applied similarly at pedestrian crossings or other hold ups. But be certain the road is clear before getting out ahead.

### Use Green Efficiently

If everybody used green to get as many as possible through each time the result in time saving would be enormous—but every little helps!

The box junction principle is excellent at lights. Equally essential is "snap" when "go" comes. Dreaming and dawdling at green by a driver can rob six of their chance to go through safely. Multiply that when two or three snails happen to be together and look how the nation's time is dissipated!

Another way to increase the numbers going through on green is for traffic to close up any unduly long gaps. Drivers should stay alert and get going when traffic moves off.

### Going fast through Green on Wide Empty "Through" Routes

Going through fast on green can be dangerous but with local knowledge of phasing, confirmed by a change to green, a brisk speed can often be safely maintained.

Very advanced driving needs brains. Getting smartly and safely through green requires skill. Not only must your eyes flash to cover both crossing roads, etc. long before reaching them, but your approaching *positioning* is vital.

It is no risk to take green at 60 m.p.h. if you know it will be green when you reach the area and there is nothing for miles.

If however the "yellow box" area has cars to its right or left, even if they are stationary, show care. Don't speed through and "cut the chrome off" the bumper of the chap on the left. His foot might slip off his clutch or brake. This happens.

If otherwise clear all round you, keep well away from him; then a brisk speed is possible, by dropping to 3rd and accelerating.

With waiting vehicles on both sides, if otherwise safe, go through the middle well clear of trouble, however remote. You thus maximize what we can call your "swerve to safety" area. But the iron rule stands:- *Never drive at a speed at which you can't stop safely in the area you see clear ahead of you.*

Keep a finger at the horn, a foot hovering over the brake. and (need I say!) the eyeballs swivelling. Alert, disciplined, fast driving can be safe. It is sleep-drivers who kill people.

The majority of green lights have to be taken at reduced speed because of traffic. Be ever alert for the maniac who comes at 80 m.p.h. when he ought to be at 28, or shoots the red in front of you.

If for some reason you can't stop in time for red (for example brake failure) and have to go through, hoot and flash lights to warn all, as the Ambulance driver would do.


## ONE-WAYS

Traffic in one-way systems—tunnels—roundabouts—etc. tends to stagnate where it meets another traffic flow.

One secret here is, where safe, to select the lane likely to have the least traffic or the fewest places where you have to "give way" to people from the right. Another secret is by knowing your road and pre-selecting a certain lane before reaching congested areas. Sometimes postponing changing lane until you have passed round bunched traffic helps. You can often get ahead without discourtesy to others.


## FIRST EXAMPLE OF THE ADVANTAGES OF USING THE LANE LEAST LIKELY TO BE HELD UP
### One-Way Underpasses

*In underpasses—Keep right.* Most underpasses have two lanes. At the exit, where other traffic joins it usually has to come in from the left. The road may have three lanes to accommodate the extra traffic or alternately precedence for underpass traffic may be established by a dotted Give-way line. Either way drivers in the left lane of the underpass need to

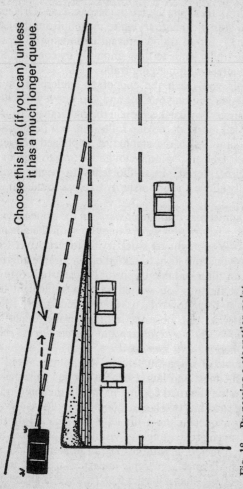

Choose this lane (if you can) unless it has a much longer queue.

Fig. 18. By-passing a stagnation point.

exercise greater care, firstly because the side wall masks the view till the last moment and secondly allowance has to be made for fools swinging across without looking.

Even when there *is* a give-way line drivers reaching it often ease over it regardless. This is bad and risky.

All this slows traffic in the left underpass lane. Drivers may even have to stop if cars are trying to push in from the left and the right lane is full of traffic, preventing moving to it.

Right lane traffic tends to flow smoothly by contrast, having less direct contact with merging traffic.

Suppose as you reach the end of an underpass, a car is travelling beside you on your left and you know you will want to turn left soon. You can keep on in the right lane because that car on your left, or if not the one following, will be almost sure to have to slow up in the stagnation explained above. This leaves the left lane empty long enough for you to ease over for your left turn. Merging-in traffic tends to begin cautiously which usually allows the opportunity to cross to the left as you pass.

All rules sometimes trap the unwary. In the same instance as above, if the left turn you want came too soon the advantages could be lost. You might get stuck trying to cross over without squeezing anyone and have to take the honourable alternative. That is go on till a suitable opportunity occurred to turn left later. Imagine the turn you wanted was at a traffic light and the queue started back towards or in the underpass; it would probably be wiser to choose the left lane in the tunnel.

*Apart from exceptions as far as possible avoid direct "conflict" with traffic merging into your road.*

The principle of by-passing stagnation points caused where lanes of traffic meet and merge can be applied to some extent when you are on the road coming in to join the main traffic, if your joining road has two lanes. Look at Fig. 18. Unless it has a much longer queue choose the left hand one. From the left you have a much greater angle of vision and thus more time to see if you can merge in without having to stop. Traffic in the right lane, usually meets emerging underpass traffic at a sharper angle and, as it also has a harder task to see, it is almost bound to have to stop or come nearer to a stop than you on the left will need. Frequently, while those on your right are stopping or have done, underpass traffic waivers with uncertainty

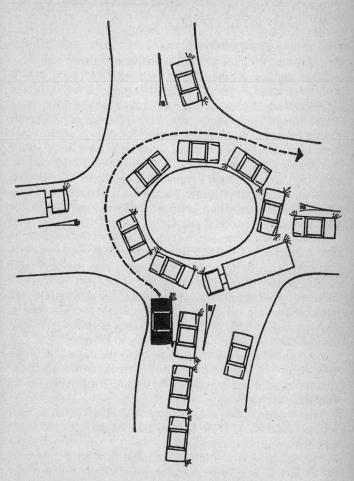

Fig. 19.   Making use of empty space at a roundabout.

leaving a gap for you to slip into once again by-passing the stagnation point.

## SECOND EXAMPLE OF USING THE LANE LEAST LIKELY TO BE HELD UP

### Multi-lane City Roundabouts

Fig. 19 is typical of a spacious modern, but traffic blocked, city roundabout. At the entry in the foreground the right lane is stuck as it has to *give way* to the solid traffic on its way round. Meanwhile there is empty space—"enough to sail the American fleet through"—round the outer circumference of almost the whole roundabout. The space is there for anyone who uses the left entry lane. I exaggerate but room exists for a driver in the left lane to get round safely, following the dotted path in Fig. 19. There is no need to move towards the middle till later, if at all. And once you are on the roundabout and a little ahead of that stagnation point at the entry, merging to the middle becomes easier, if required.

If you wish to transfer to the lane next to the edge of the roundabout island there is no obligation to do so at an early stage. Without being too clever you can "play it along" as it were. *Variation of speed is the key, and be sure that traffic ahead has not stopped*; a touch of acceleration in the appropriate gear often allows safe switching ahead of another car. Conversely, decelerating with a touch of brake may enable you to slip behind another car without discourtesy to anyone.

After entering by the left lane to avoid the stagnation of the right hand one, sometimes your only reason for moving to the middle is to avoid stagnation at future entry where more traffic is pushing in.

The advanced driver uses opportunities with skill but without risk or discourtesy. If he fails to take his chances the worst punishment is going round again.

By good driving you filter ahead and with art should have (a) caused no one to be held up, (b) avoided adding to the congestion, and (c) released the space you would have occupied for another.

I can visualize members of some road safety committees leaping from their seats in rage. But as every house built for sale, *at whatever price*, releases another for someone perhaps less fortunate, so one aim of very advanced driving is the relief of every road space to promote the progress of all.

If you are no longer there you are not holding anyone up. Some may be jealous of the advantage you have gained but education should teach that jealousy is childish.

There is no need to be unfair. You must not take advantage of others who have positioned by the "accepted" rules. All you are doing is keeping out of their motoring lives by better driving.

An opposite effect to that described in Fig. 19 may happen at city roundabouts and a slightly different technique is useful.

As Fig. 20 shows traffic halts instead, in two queues mainly on the left, aggravated by the front vehicle in the right hand of these queues having pulled too far to his left. (He was attempting to join the left stream). This leaves room on his right for an expert. As the last of any group of vehicles coming from the right passes the nose of the expert's car there will be a brief moment while the rear of that vehicle still blocks the badly positioned amateur. This is just about to occur in Fig. 20. It is now that the expert deftly slots his car forward tucked behind the passing vehicle and away. He gets straight to the island edge lane in the process.

Snags may prevent this being possible but it is often useful. One snag is if someone steps across the neck of the approach road from the left, coinciding with the moment in question. Then the expert has a fractionally longer wait while the walker passes, and loses ground, but it was worth a try.

Sometimes such techniques would be unreasonable or too aggressive. Always temper enthusiasm with fair play. If others *are* making use of gaps the Advanced Driver waits.

Where others keep failing to grasp their gaps (you recognise after following a while) you have to consider the greatest benefit for the greatest number.

## THIRD EXAMPLE OF USING THE LANE LEAST LIKELY TO BE HELD UP
### The "Road Narrows" Problem

One-ways often narrow unexpectedly. The same can happen at the end of dual carriageways. You sometimes find two lanes in your direction on an ordinary road are whittled down to one with little warning. You have to watch, well ahead of arriving,

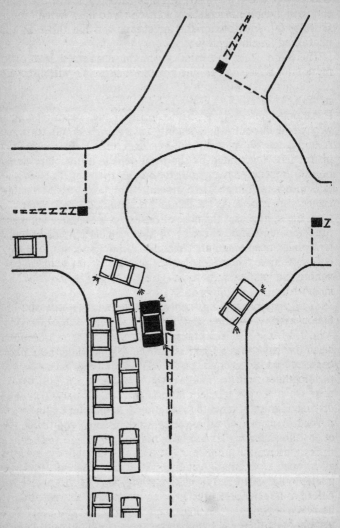

Fig. 20. Another roundabout technique.

which side reduces width and which edge remains straight. Unless you selected the straight side earlier you will probably end with a choice of crushing someone who has "laned" more skilfully (at your own risk!) or stopping while those in the unaffected lane sweep by.

There are other instances where the unaffected lane technique wins as the reader who grasps the principle will discover.

## APPROACHING ONE-WAY STREETS

It is essential, if obvious, to look left *first* when reaching a one-way which flows *T*-wise across your road from left to right. A check to the right for walkers is essential. The ingrained instruction "look right, left and right again" must be reversed here. Otherwise that naughty habit of beginning to nose out once you see it is clear right and during the moment of turning the head to look left, can result in a big bang *from the left*.

Where a one-way forms the stem of a T leading *Off* your road there is often a "Pass Either Side" arrows bollard placed at the entrance. Many drivers nevertheless enter the one-way *only* into its left lane. They seem to see but not believe. Advanced drivers pass by such people, by using the road as instructed.

The same drivers will often be found wrongly positioned for turning right when they reach the T at the other end of the one-way. This does not matter if the road to be entered is one-way but if it is two-way and they pull up on the left, while they wait, they succeed in frustrating any following left turners who are positioned correctly. They also look angry if you pull up on their right properly, ready to go right! Avoid such amateur driving. The right edge of these streets should be treated as if it was the crown of the road by those turning right. Let me expose another way time is lost by this.

Both directions of traffic crossing the T politely stop to allow such a wrongly positioned right turner to exit. Because people only wait briefly (incidentally part II of the problem), before some relentless urge to go seems to take charge, anyone baulked behind the amateur and waiting to get away left usually finds there isn't time to move up and come out before main road traffic is again under way. He should have been able to turn left simultaneously and only occupying the same time space. Instead what will probably now have to happen is another group of main road drivers having to stop to let him out. Time is thus wasted for many more drivers.

## TRAFFIC FLOW
I have emphasised traffic flow principles and how much we need them. Please believe that *even on our busy roads*, twice as much traffic could flow smoothly and efficiently, if everyone acted for the benefit of the greatest number.

## EASY-WAY FOR ONE-WAYS
In a one-way, in the event of a scrape, it is usually hard to prove guilt. The dangerous lane is usually the middle one, with vehicles belting along either side you are busy watching them, and have less time to look out in front.

It is safer to keep to one edge as far as possible. Stay close enough to prevent a cyclist imagining he could squeeze between you and the pavement and about half your problems are eliminated. Don't go so close to the kerb as to damage tyres. Shopping crowds and jay walkers are another risk but where they occur it is normal for traffic to lower speed. You also have to watch you are not squeezed into the pavement.

If you have to stay in a central lane for any distance, keep in mind the "Stop or slow in preference to swerving" advice. The extreme right on long one-ways is normally quicker and safer because Buppy drivers tend to crowd and struggle on the left. In showery weather, sometimes only the more used left lane dries out and for safety it is always wiser to use it, if empty.

\* \* \*

## TOWN STREETS
*In contrast with the main "through" roads, you find in the town streets, on suburban roads and back streets, roads which are usually only one lane each way. These are sometimes a maze of parked vehicles, blind crossroads, roadworks and the other mass junk of suburbia, not to mention their death rôle in and near residential areas which may be children's (unofficial) playgrounds.*

## KEEPING YOUR DISTANCE
This section, together with the notes under "Bringing science to sight" (page 43) forms perhaps the outstanding instruction of safe driving which I have been able to express.

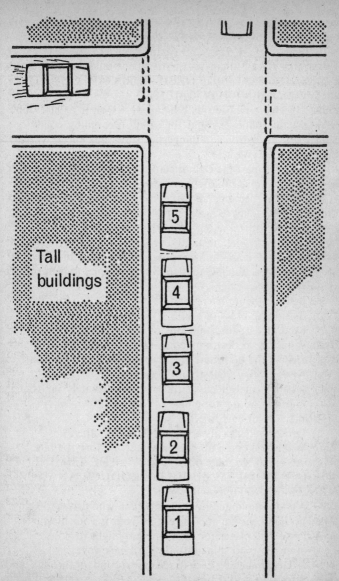

Fig. 21. Four Madmen.

Alas, one can't recommend specified distances for drivers spacing themselves behind vehicles ahead. A safe gap cannot be based on speed. It is not a gap related to speed which is important. Such an approximate rule would be dangerous compared to the crucial NEED FOR GAP VARIATION FROM MOMENT TO MOMENT.

Many drivers realise this but fail to act on it or else don't have the discipline essential for safety. Prevailing conditions alter every few yards and dangerous situations ahead increase or reduce in degree.

Leaving a gap of the right distance, plus stopping room, is a repeating process; rapidly increasing the gap at every danger risk, however fleeting, allowing it to shorten only as risks diminish. You may reduce the gap for other reasons, perhaps preparing to overtake, but only when safe.

Extending the gap instantly widens your angle of vision, provides yards extra for stopping, and reduces the need for split-second reactions. Gap increasing examples (which should be instinctive):

a) Before a bend or corner.
b) Before the brow of a hill.
c) Near crossroads, junctions or traffic lights.
d) Wherever pedestrians congregate to give you a chance against the odd idiot, drunk or child who jumps out.
e) Approaching Pedestrian Crossings.
f) When traffic ahead of the man immediately in front is knotting up or stopping.
g) If the road narrows.
h) Parked vehicles ahead one side or the other.
i) When you come up behing a big van, lorry or bus.

The list could go on; BASICALLY—THE IMMINENCE OF *ANY* PROBLEM SHOULD PRODUCE AN APPROPRIATE REACTION—BY YOU.

Don't be intimidated by the car behind who drives too close. The gap between you and the car in front is your life-saver.

A list of safe places for reducing gap might read:

a) after the road splits into dual carriageway;
b) if the car ahead is easy to see over, round, or through, and obviously well driven;
c) where buildings are back from the road or railings fence off any children. The list could continue.

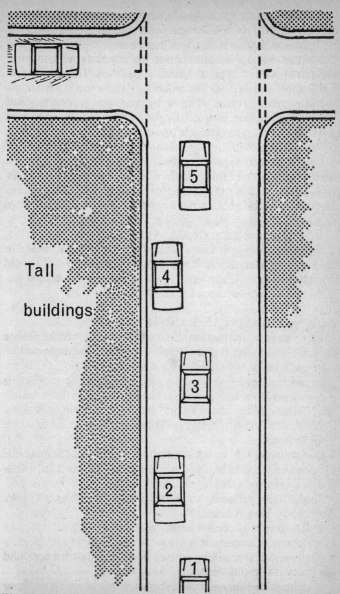

Tall

buildings

5

4

3

2

1

Fig. 22.   Five sane men.

To re-emphasise (and this is rarely stressed) the secret is VARIATION . . . the bigger the risk the longer the gap. *And More and More so as speed increases.*

Think of the gap you must constantly adjust as the "stopping and thinking gap". Fig. 21 shows 4 madmen. The 5th is sane but helpless at the front. The crossroads at the top is a frightening blind danger area. The 4 by keeping nose-to-tail are *restricting* their own view of any risks and if No. 5 had to jam on (as he well may) a 6-vehicle pile up would be almost certain.

Compare this with the wisdom and vision of the wise drivers in Fig. 22 as they approach the same situation.

They understand "thinking time". The time-lag between the moment the chap in front brakes (or crashes) and your reaction. Each, by increasing his "stopping and thinking" gap, and/or by positioning to one side of the line taken by the car ahead, is leaving himself room to stop in.

I have never seen it said that keeping away from danger is the heart of safety. Even if the danger is $\frac{1}{2}$ a mile off. At the first sniff of trouble the very advanced driver will extend his gap so removing any need for panic-station action.

## HOW A SIGNAL CAN BANISH DOUBT

Imagine your main road bends where another of similar width goes straight on. At first you think your road is straight on but then the back of the Give Way notice or a tell-tale line shows that you have right of way to swing round the bend. Fig. 23 shows this with a car arriving at the Give Way point towards you. Because of the layout he may conclude you will be forking left and with no other traffic on the main road decide to come straight on out.

One way to avoid an accident is to drive so that the position of your vehicle tells him you are going round, but it is worth giving a brief indicator signal. This removes doubt, alerts, and advises. The positioning technique would be Advanced; plus the signal—Very Advanced!

If the chap still doesn't seem to understand (and this may apply at any side road where someone seems only to be looking the other way) you will be wise to hoot and hoot till he looks your way. Meantime watch his front wheels.

If there is continuous traffic from his left while someone looking the other way, this makes it unlikely he will mo

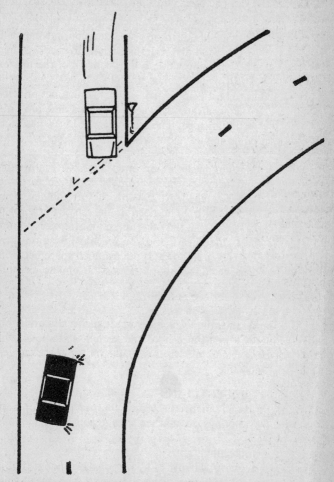

Fig. 23.   Positioning, *and* a signal, to alert a driver in doubt.
The two main points discussed in the text are, 1) the need for
a brief signal, 2) positioning so it is obvious where you are
going.

What may be dangerous is if he sees there will soon be a gap
—the joy may cause him to shoot forward before he checks and
sees you!

## DO YOU ALWAYS LOOK UNDER PARKED CARS?

We learn to watch below parked vehicles for feet, prams, etc.,
and check for anyone about to open the door but few manage
to always do it. The good driver grabs chances to check as they
arise. Seizing these fleeting views is a trademark of the master
as explained in "Bringing Science to Sight", page 43.

But there has to be an alternative because sometimes priority
for the eyes to concentrate elsewhere coincides and prevents
such chances being grasped. The alternative: SLOW DOWN.
The sub-conscious should shout it to you; *give yourself time*,
instead.

Some drawings emphasise an example. Fig. 24(a) shows the
tell-tale feet and tricycle wheels from 50 yards, before the
parked estate car is reached. At 25 yards they are hidden from
the driver as in Fig. 24(b). The horrible unseen struggle for a
scooter is in (c), seen from the other direction. If you have not
had time to check underneath and you reach (b) position then
(1) SLOW DOWN, (2) HOOT, (3) put as much space between
you and the car when passing as is possible in the circumstances.

### Hooting On Behalf Of Others

When coming the other way and you see such a situation you
may save life by a well-timed hoot and keeping in to your own
side to leave the oncoming driver who has yet to see the danger
a swerving and safety gap.

## SWARMING PEDESTRIANS

Sometimes hundreds of people crowd the road near football
grounds, race meetings, in market streets, etc. To help nose
through:
  a) Switch on headlights.
  b) Politely request "Thank You" out of the window.
  c) Hold the clutch down and *gear in neutral*, rev the engine
     . . . brroom! brrrroom! brrrrooom! Don't hoot. That's not
     "cricket". Humour is your best bet. After all, you can't
     mow them down! Rightly or not they feel they have as
     much right on the street as you.

view at 50 yards

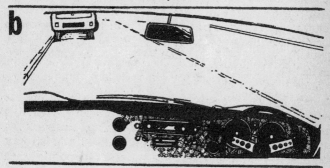

nothing looks amiss
at 25 yards

view from the other
direction

Fig. 24. Looking under parked cars.

# HIDDEN MONSTERS

At a crossroad, imagine going straight on up the main road when an approaching vehicle risks turning right across you just ahead. *Most Dangerous!* You brake to just miss the idiot without realizing motor-bike(s) or smaller cars are hidden from you behind that vehicle who may commit themselves to swing across you as well, *leaving little chance to avoid a smash.* You are Not blameless; you ought to have been SLOW ENOUGH to allow for this unseen risk till you knew it did not exist.

# BLIND SPOTS

The natural blind spot of the eye in relation to driving has received little publicity. Fig. 25 demonstrates it if you try the test explained. This means you can easily look without seeing, in certain directions.

Further blind spots are due to door pillars, mirrors or driving licence holders. Dirt or greasy smears left on the screen or side

Look at the steering wheel on the *right*, and close your right eye. Hold the book about a foot away from your *left* eye, straight in front of it. At Approximately this distance it is impossible to see the wheel on the left while your eye focusses on the one on the right. The distance may be slightly more, or less, depending on your eyes. This shows there is a considerable angle of view which the eye cannot cover—a built in eye blind spot.

Fig. 25.   Natural eye blind spots.

windows may seem nothing but can also lead to disaster by limiting vision, especially on wet nights. A hanging dolly or stupid stickers front, side or back are practically criminal.

This is why at junctions one quick look and away is not enough. *It is the second (or even third) look that picks out anything missed previously.* I CANNOT OVERSTRESS THE ADVICE "A SECOND LOOK PICKS OUT ANY VEHICLE HIDDEN PREVIOUSLY" so I will repeat it again.

---

A second look picks out anything hidden previously

---

It is imperative that you look long enough. You must look sufficiently to see movement. You must not be ashamed, or too lazy, to swivel the head, neck and shoulders forward, back, any way necessary to avoid (for lack of a better word) being "blind-spotted". If your neck is too stiff with age, retire from driving.

In heavy rain, drops on the side windows mask vision, so open sufficiently to see. Open more at night, when seeing is harder.

Fig. 26 illustrates how, because it is close to the eye, even a small part of the car such as the door pillar which is creating a blind spot, can obscure a wide area.

## SYSTEMIZING A SAFETY EYE APPROACH TO JUNCTIONS

You are not on the main road so we will not differentiate between approaching a Give Way line, a Stop line, or no line. We are concerned with safety vision. We will assume you have used your mirror.

Your street is narrow. Buildings, billboards, hedges etc. at the corners where you meet the crossing road, make the opening blind.

With an open-to-view crossroad opportunities to look one or both ways while approaching would have been taken as they arose. Here—the blind corner—may be a black spot.

### The Deadly Blind Corner

In the last few yards speed is dropped to walking, no more—in the last 5 feet to a snail's pace. Immediate dangers are likely in the final 10–15 feet before the stopping position. The dance of death usually comes from the left—prams, children racing,

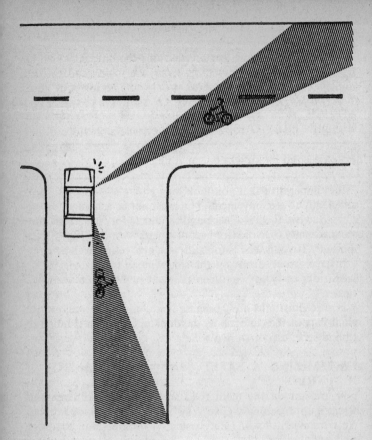

Fig. 26. Door pillar blind spot.

youths, dogs, etc. In a flash one may be under you, crushed.

Your devastating braking reaction must beat them to it.
*The blinder the slower* is the motto. You may literally need to
stop, allow a second or two for people to note the bonnet and
hope they may hear the engine, and then only, edge forward
gently till you see more.

The danger may be less from the right but if anyone is
walking across safety and courtesy demand that he has
priority. Another right side danger may come from what I
term the "kerbside crawler". The sort who tootle along picking

up the nails in the gutter and pass inches from your stopping line; or perhaps a moped.

A real danger, while you are reaching the line, may also be from the left; someone coming along the main road to turn right into your road, who unashamedly cuts across your nose. *This is a frequent type of accident*. Prevention is to watch and stop, in time.

In the "blind" drive entrance to our home a previous owner told me two cars "met" and 5 people were taken to hospital.

Systemizing approach to dangerous crossroads is not merely "Looking right, left and right again" and in the mirror. Such simplified advice was fine 25 years ago.

To-day the all embracing method of integrating this roll stop with efficient anti-blind spot treatment is needed. Every conceivable danger point must be seen by moving head and eyes, taking priorities in order, during the last 12 feet.

The driver from the left who cuts across you as he whirls right *without having signalled* is another serious trap. Suppose you reached the crossing and are waiting for the only car in sight to pass. It is tootling along from the left. The intention to turn right is unknown because the driver hasn't signalled nor noticeably positioned or slowed. He is one of the 50% of road fools.

With every direction clear, and expecting him to pass on the other side any second, you move into your half of the main road simultaneously with your final look right. Then things happen! You may be turning right or going straight over but your naughty habit of moving out like this makes you part 2 of the smash. You've guessed? As you were edging out he was cutting over and, Bang! Two idiots meet. If they survive they will not make this common blunder again. Why do it in the first place? Note that seat-belts are unlikely to help you in such side crashes.

## THE DANGER OF STALLING

A feeling of well being takes hold of many a driver as he sails along the main road. Despite a vehicle emerging from a side road ahead, he continues at his set speed, oblivious to the chance that that driver might stall. If only he would lift his foot off, many accidents would be avoided.

*Question—How can such idiocy be avoided?*

*Answer—NEVER stall at all.*

1) Be sure you have more than enough acceleration to give power to mount the camber (if any) of the main road.

2) *Get your accelerator going before, as, and after you let the clutch up, so that you will get over the danger area safely, quickly.* Use resolute (but not ferocious) acceleration, always.

If using the handbrake keep your hand on it so you cannot forget to take it off. Same with the choke, ready to pull or push it if required. With both—be really careful. If the gear or car shudders stop quickly if safe—was it in third instead of first?

Never linger in danger areas or begin to cross till sure you *will* succeed and cannot be robbed of a space to occupy beyond, out of danger.

If people behind are tooting, it only annoys you if you let it. But be fair because few hoot without reason. They may think you are dreaming instead of concentrating.

Wait for a gap with time to cross at walking speed. You go faster, but need that safety margin. I stress that the *killer is stalling in the face of the main road traffic*.

Keep your eyes switching left, right and ahead and to where ever danger may lurk, *while crossing*.

When driving along the main road and you see someone ahead pulling across apparently in plenty of time it pays to think (not like the wandering mind erratic buppy, or the "my speed" types mentioned in chapter 1) "Is he going to STALL?". Working on the assumption he *will*, until it is clear he *has not*, will force you to ease speed early. This is the key that enables you to stop in time should the worst happen, which it frequently does.

In the event of an accident at least some of the blame is likely to be laid at your door. In recent court cases concerned with this type of crash the prosecution's view that, because "you should always be able to stop within the distance you can see to be clear" and therefore it must be partly your fault, has been upheld. In the verdict a percentage of blame is attributed to each party, 20% of it, for example, having to be accepted by the main road driver.

## POSITIONING—SAFETY'S SUPREME ALLY

Partly summing up this section on Town Streets one can reflect that *"positioning", that is anticipation and getting into the correct part of the road, is, for safety, of greater importance than signals.*

I would rather drive a million miles with a driver who knew this than ten with one who had disc brakes, safety belts, new tyres etc., but did not grasp this need.

*Equally important is disciplining speed to the conditions.*

## STOPPING AND PARKING

When pulling into the side, your position gently easing towards the kerb and slowing down should be enough to tell others what you are doing. A left flasher however confirms it. If a nearby turning could confuse an arm slow-down signal helps, but usually it is wiser not to stop, however briefly, near a corner.

In shopping areas, gaps between cars are harder to fit into. The sequence for tackling the problem the right way for a one car space is shown in steps by Fig. 27.

When a space is more than two car lengths you can go in forwards and shunt into your final position later. This saves traffic behind waiting while you manoeuvre.

Sometimes when you have stopped a little forward of a one car space and are trying to reverse in drivers pull up too close. You are prevented before you've started! To avoid this, stop initially *before* reaching the gap. Don't move forward till the chap behind has stopped. Then, when you nip forward smartly to your starting position (a) in Fig. 27, he should be able to see what you are doing and wait courteously.

Occasionally some cheeky follower seizes the opportunity to drive forward into your space. If this is done intentionally, it is better to treat it with contempt. It is not worth delaying traffic to have a row.

## PEDESTRIANS ARE CRACKERS

It might be said "a pedestrian is one who does not know a car can reverse". When you are reversing shoppers are frequently stupid enough to walk through the decreasing gap between you and the car you are backing up to. *THEY EXPECT YOU TO*

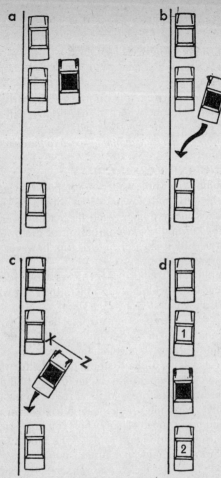

a) Stop beyond the space, parallel to and with the back of your car slightly ahead of the back of the car next the space. There should be about 3 feet between your car and the other one.

b) Reverse in, very slowly does it, left lock to begin with, but not too deeply.

c) Begin to change steering lock from the line X—Z and aim to be on full lock just as soon as possible after your left front wing clears the parked car.

d) Once "in", adjust to leave equal room in front and behind so that cars 1, and 2, can get out easily.

Fig. 27. Parking between cars.

*HAVE SEEN THEM*. Show care if reversing with people about because you would be blamed if you hit anyone.

## MOTTO FOR REVERSING—DON'T
*Don't unless you must*. Reversing is an unpleasant necessity and because of its dangers wise drivers reverse as little as possible.

When forced to reverse, move backwards *only enough to make the next forward move, never more*. NOT ONE INCH MORE.

On the other hand, it is often better to reverse into an opening instead of having to reverse out when you leave. Spaces in car parks, and driveways are examples.

If you have taken a wrong road and want to turn back the plan might be to pull up past an opening and reverse into it. Safer however would be to turn in an easier place somewhere along a quiet side road.

Some so-called advanced drivers rely solely on the mirrors when reversing. This is crazy as mirrors don't show everything, especially small children.

# 4
# *Country Techniques*

## OUR SMALLER COUNTRY ROADS
### Really Narrow Lanes

*Picture the typical narrow road, barely wider than the car, usually sunken and with high grass banks or hedges. Here are to be found the week-end drivers or the over-confident local who knows every blade of grass and has driven along there 1,000 times!*

Fig. 28 illustrates a blind hairpin bend without passing room. Unless you and any car approaching both crawl, on reaching the bend itself, it will be almost impossible to prevent a smash. As a sensible person you would always have slowed to snail's pace at such a corner. Fine if others were equally responsible.

The skilled driver however realizes that anything, including the incredible, can and does happen and that the normally sane sometimes do crazy things. The young especially will not always submit to the discipline that wisdom dictates.

In such circumstances, because there is so little evasion or safety margin to swerve into, each driver must hoot and do so long and often enough to be heard before and during the bend. He must tuck in to his own side and cover the brake during the blindest areas. It only remains to pray that any approaching driver is not deaf or mad!

You thus give yourself the chance to stop on the proverbial sixpence. The reason for keeping right in, even if it only leaves a foot or so to your offside, is to give any downhill cyclist, such as in Fig. 28, with his head down, room to scrape by and survive.

Remember that question on accident insurance claim forms: "Did you sound your horn?" which shows the importance those with daily experience of accidents attach to this safety measure. Don't listen to those who say that in some areas abroad horns are prohibited. Such places do not necessarily have our weight of traffic, narrow lanes or habits.

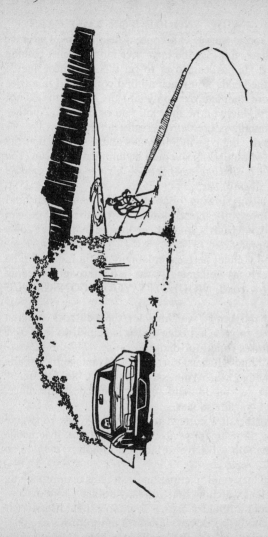

Fig. 28. A blind hairpin bend.

Never rely on the horn. It won't clear the road. Imagine a herd of cows at a blind bend. They keep coming regardless!

## ROADS JUST WIDE ENOUGH FOR TWO CARS

Seemingly innocent curves can conceal death traps. One rare but frightening example is the boy-racer motor cyclist coming the other way. He has leant over to get the straightest line he can through the bend. You reach a blind corner and in a trice he's there, more than half over on your side. Although it is not your fault, if he hits you he may kill you or himself. Another dangerous example is the delivery van running late. . . .

It is no use driving on winding roads and assuming that the only problem you might meet could be another small car. *You must be ready to find the devil seeking his opportunity and he could be in a steam roller!*

This often means slowing for corners more than fools behind might like. Once you can see along the next straight you can accelerate to your heart's content or slow up and let the fools go by, if you prefer.

If you killed a child, perhaps coming out of a hidden bridle path, as quickly as you might swat a fly through speeding along a narrow road, WOULDN'T YOUR CONSCIENCE BLEED?

For right hand bends, watching for the odd rock sticking out, keep close to your left edge and it is helpful to lean over to your left to see round for danger.

Entering a blind left bend there is an advantage in keeping out from the edge, when your speed is reasonable. Oncomers see you earlier, as you do them and you see pedestrians, dogs, etc., on your own side sooner.

If doing this be slow enough to brake and ready to swerve into your side, allowing for weather and conditions. If someone is approaching you will have to move in rapidly. *You have no right to rob his road.*

In country lanes you sometimes meet streams of approaching traffic. As well as watching that you may not have to move out slightly to avoid a boulder or tree root, you should scan their side for the same. The driver who cares more for his car than for you will swing over for the smallest pothole. Depending on space available you may have to slow up or stop. In narrow conditions grip the wheel tightly then if you misjudge and hit a rock you will be less likely to bounce off into worse danger. In tight circumstances keep your car parallel if you can with the approaching vehicle to ease passing.

Sometimes on a narrow road such as we have been discussing you find yourself nearing the brow of a hill, or perhaps a corner, when suddenly a motor bike approaches with a car close on its heels about to pass it. Supposing that the road is too narrow for all three of you, you must be prepared to *act*, even though it may not "theoretically" be up to you to give way. It depends upon speeds and circumstances but if someone is going to need to brake sharply to avoid an accident it is usually safer if you can do so, rather than the chap breathing on the motor-cycle exhaust pipe. If he brakes he may slide—into the motor-cycle, or *into you*. If the bike *brakes* as well, matters could rapidly get worse; whereas if you *brake* and "positionally" show what you are doing by nosing tight into your side: (a) it allows seconds extra thinking and dropping back time for the on-coming car and (b) it removes doubt from a dangerous situation, especially for the motor-cyclist, (and he has the least control over what may happen).

In any similar circumstance make it your rule to give way if it's easier and safer for you than for the others.

### Crossroads In Country Lanes

Country crossroads are often not marked for priority so assume neither road has it. Stop till sure it is safe. To maximise vision lie out a little when blind to the left but clear to see right or keep left if the right is more obscured. This is the advanced art of manufacturing extra vision by positioning. A hoot as you start across can save you from the unforseeable.

## MAIN ROADS CROSSING THE COUNTRYSIDE
*Now wider roads: the A and B routes varying between ample two way width, three lanes (two-way) and occasional dual carriageways:*

## LEAVING ROOM FOR OTHERS TO OVERTAKE
Suppose you are part of a traffic stream with no wish to over-take. As stream speed increases you should allow those in front away to leave space for faster traffic to pass you. If a bunch of selfish nose-to-tail drivers forms, faster cars can only pass at

risk to themselves and *the others*. Behind a lorry, they may have to plod for miles. All must be patient and wait for a safe moment but if the driver immediately behind the lorry has a slow car he should drop back allowing faster cars to "leap-frog" him one by one as they pass the lorry. Consideration for others is the essence of good driving.

Even if the overtaking car does not use the gap it must be left at his disposal. Otherwise the driver who did not leave it could be part III of an accident.

Part II of such an accident would probably be an oncoming motorist who stuck to his "rights" and gave no leeway to the overtaking driver. The original fault would be with the over-taking driver for failing to make sure he had a clear passage to pass *and a gap to go into* but apportioning blame to the dead is a useless task!

Even more to blame, because he could have done something about it, would be the fool who insisted on his rights.

At first sight of such a situation he ought to have instantly signalled left, pulled into his side and braked, if need be, to a stop.

Instantaneous braking in danger gets the car balanced and under control for that second later when real danger may exist. One is ready for necessary evasive action perhaps even driving off the road to the left. If there was a high kerb this would necessitate a tight grip on the wheel and mounting the kerb at an angle to prevent being kicked back. Do anything to avoid the head-on killer.

The immediate left indicator signal: (a) tells the oncoming nutcase you have seen him and (b) you will be pulling in to the left. You thus decide for him which way *he* must turn and you probably give him confidence he will need to pass through the danger he has created.

## THE NIGHTMARE THREE LANES, TWO-WAY
*Including many wide roads which, although marked as ONE LANE each way, are used like the three lane roads.*

### Bends to the Right
On a right bend stay well over in the left of the three lanes. This keeps you away from trouble if heavy traffic is coming the other way. It gives earlier vision of any fool coming who is bent

on passing on the corner and who is otherwise masked by the leading traffic. Where another driver in front of you goes round with his car in the middle of the road (or a madman overtakes you) keep well left and a long way behind him, to allow yourself a space to keep out of any accident.

On the other hand, at a right hand bend sometimes, visibility shows all is clear for half a mile and this gives the good driver a really safe chance to pass.

## Bends to the Left

Keep well left but not so close that if you have to pass a cyclist you need to swing out. Keeping too close in may tempt someone to overtake at a dangerous time. If someone does try be ready to brake or accelerate as required, to let him cut back to save his life and maybe yours!

## Disappearing Gap

If an overtaker's gap is closing because traffic ahead is stopping but he is determined to pass, you may have to brake heavily to keep a gap for him. Who was right or wrong matters not. Survival has supremacy.

When someone cuts in front of you for whatever reason, *don't accelerate—let him in*, slowing down if need. Only madmen accelerate and *cause head on, death accidents, killing innocent and guilty*. If a van or lorry is passing flash headlights to show him in his mirror just as soon as he can safely cut in. The driver otherwise has an awful job to know when he is clear and you may not see what danger is forcing him in. It could involve you too.

## Double White Lines

Crossing a line you shouldn't is breaking the law. If the line is *continuous your* side, you are not allowed to go over it. You would only cross a line against you to avoid an accident or pass round a stationary obstruction.

When you are "inside" a double line and have to pass a cyclist, or small obstruction, use your indicator. Drivers react slowly and follow blindly when they know overtaking is banned so this wakes them up. It's extra important at night and also useful where there are no double lines if the road is narrow.

Fig. 29 shows an arrangement of double lines which some-

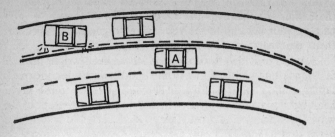

**Driver A, LOOK OUT ! for driver B**

Fig. 29.   Illusory double white lines.

times replaces a free for all of two-way traffic on three lanes.
It's easy to be lulled into thinking no one will come out of the
single lane, when you are in the outer passing lane of the two
lane side. The *single lane* has a dotted line on its side entitling
drivers to come out if safe. Alas some come out when it is
unsafe. The moral is to keep alive, keep alert.


## HERRING BONE LINES
Diagonal lines are sometimes marked on a main road as in
Fig. 30 where there is a turning off. They form an elongated
island which most drivers guess creates a no-man's land. The
lines round the edge however have gaps so one *can* go on the
striped area. It is better not to because the island is intended to
keep the area clear for those turning right, so they will not be
hit in the back or by anyone coming.

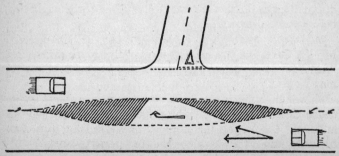

Fig. 30.   Herring bone lines.

But, when moving into the "shielded" right turn position, the earlier you get over the easier it is for followers to filter past on your left and to see your signal in good time. For this there is no harm in running on the striped area.

Shelter is provided by these areas for the deadly right turn off fast roads but while waiting in the middle watch for the over-taking maniac, approaching or behind; be ready to use horn, head lights, flash brake lights or in the last resort, drive out of the way. On a high speed road where you haven't the help of the herring-bone lines be on special guard. Keep your front wheels straight ahead while waiting. Then, if shunted: at least it will not be into oncoming traffic.

Herring bones are of immense safety value if used correctly.

## WHERE SIDE ROADS CROSS MAIN ONES

FACT: Few drivers heed crossroad warning signs and main road traffic moves fast. It includes some sleep-drivers. You court death if you risk delay during crossing so be sure *your accelerator is really going before, as and after you release the clutch*, and that you have enough power to reach safety. Avoid being caught in the middle at all costs and NEVER DRIVE ACROSS ANYONE'S SAFE STOPPING DISTANCE.

If a car waits opposite to come straight over you can both cross at once. But if he is turning right he has to go round behind you in theory, as at any cross road, whether you are going right or across. In practice, many attempt to beat you by nipping across your bows. Situations vary but this is likely when main road traffic from the left clears before that from the right—which holds you at the edge of your road. The chap opposite grabs the chance to get half-way out for his right turn before you can move.

You must establish if he will do this BEFORE YOU MOVE. Otherwise you may get tied together in the middle and "fastards" on the main road, *not realizing you are both in a fix*, may hit you.

Showing the fellow a straight on or right turn signal before traffic clears ought to prevent trouble, but he may pay no attention. Should you therefore get tied in a knot, you must be ready, unless there road is clear, to reverse to safety.

Some non-thinking Buppy behind may have closed up by

this time. Right! Reverse into the *off-side* of the side road if necessary, but get *off* the major road.

When both you and a man waiting opposite are going *right* you can "positionally" and manually by a signal advise him you are ready when the chance comes to pass him left side to

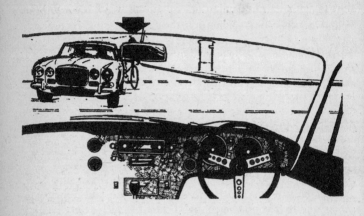

Fig. 31. Positional driving.

left side to save time. Fig. 31 shows one danger of this, how-ever; you must look out for any cyclist behind him.

## HOW IT MAY BE POSSIBLE TO SAVE TIME WHEN YOU JOIN A MAIN ROAD

Where the entry to a main road is wide and the view both ways is open as you reach the junction it may be safe to move on to the main road without a stop. Often readiness to do this saves minutes. For example by keeping going you may be able to join the road ahead of a slow car safely. Had you stopped first, in the few seconds lost the car would have become too close. Behind the slow car could be a long stream. But look out!—when turning *left* someone *from that direction* may be in the process of overtaking and coming fast on *your* side of the road.

The technique at such junctions is to *cut speed earlier than usual* during your approach to the line. About 20 yards from it your speed should be little more than walking pace. This gives you time for advance glances to confirm if it will be safe to turn without a stop. If clear a few yards are still left in which to re-gather speed. Otherwise it is easy to stop.

Sometimes leaving yourself room for re-gathering speed enables you to "tail" into a longish gap which would be impossible after a stop.

This needs skill, the right gear, and extreme watchfulness that in your enthusiasm to get on to the main road without stopping you still see every danger.

## VILLAGES OUT IN COUNTRY ROUTES

A few main roads still have to pass through quaint old villages. Ancient hanging signs or picturesque corners of buildings may lean out above a road still as narrow as a century ago. One expects "snarl-ups" to occur but they are made much worse by drivers who sit in the queue with their motoring-minds vacant.

Queues in both directions sometimes seem to get "interlocked". Both become stuck in such a way that until the blockage is released at one end, no-one can move at the other. For example a lorry may be unable to squeeze through a very narrow part of a street until a car in the other direction has moved on. But the car cannot move on because of a similar bottleneck ahead of him at the other end of the jam.

A few alert drivers can usually save the situation. One hopes no advanced driver would ever wedge his car into a bottleneck. But suppose a jam happens and you are caught somewhere in one of the queues in the middle. Keep a look out further up the line, and behind you. Frequently, by moving a few inches on or back, into the edge or onto the pavement, you can allow the cars nearest you to move as well. A small movement can make it possible for someone stuck along the line to release himself and in turn for the blockage to clear. Once one "end" of a bottleneck is released the other is usually clear soon.

So don't sit there staring at brake lights or the doll behind— think what you can do to get things moving! You might persuade a Buppy who thinks his car is 9 feet wide by mild gesticulating! It often pays to get out and hand-wave nervous drivers through a safe space.

## TALKING AND LOOKING AT THE COUNTRYSIDE

Some people can talk happily *and concentrate* on driving simultaneously, but others cannot. You have to judge your capacity honestly. Even the brilliant at it need to quit conversing during difficult situations.

Gazing at the scenery (or birds by the road) is taboo, as well as suicidal. If you "must" do it restrict yourself to fleeting glances taken while the road ahead is clear for miles and straight. Never look away more than a second at a time. That way you are likely only to kill yourself.

## "GUESSWORK" NAVIGATION

Fix in your mind before starting the relative position of each town you go to as compared with the previous and the next and you shouldn't miss the road even if you miss the sign. Knowing that town "Y" is way down to the left of town "X" on the map enables you to pick the relative out of town road "blind-fold". Passengers marvel how you always seem to know!

## SUMMARY OF POLICY

1) Systemize the way you watch each relevant detail and hazard as you approach it. If your main road flows across another side road you still need to watch. When you cannot see right at first but the left has open view, check the left. This leaves you free to look right the moment you can. The secret is looking in the right places at the right time.

2) If you do not have sufficient vision YOU MUST SLOW UP.

3) With other cars ahead as you all approach a hazard, discipline yourself to maintain enough safety margin around *you*. Increase your "thinking and stopping" gap perhaps, or keep to one side of the line taken by whoever is immediately ahead. Both disciplines let you see more, and both "manufacture" stopping room.

PLAN THE WAY YOU READ THE ROAD.

IF NEEDED ADJUST YOUR POSITIONING.

IF THE ABOVE ARE NOT ENOUGH—SLOW UP.

The faster you drive the greater the importance of instant braking to bring the car under control at the first suspicion of a hazard. THE HARD THING IS STOPPING FOR DANGER but if you have begun to stop and the car is in braking equilibrium, it is easier. Your job is to avoid smashes. *Remember a hoot in time may change disaster into breathing space.*

KEEP A "COCOON" OF SAFE-AREA ALL AROUND YOU. This is one of the great safety messages and the size of your safety "cocoon" will depend on the speed of your reactions, make of car etc. It will be different for each person.

# 5

# *Overtaking*

*Never try to pass in this world by risking passing into the next.*

The secret of overtaking is to vizualise in advance every detail of what might happen during the operation.

## REDUCE TIME EXPOSURE TO DANGER
Experience proves that the minimum exposure to danger, i.e. the least time on the off, wrong, side of the road, should be the aim at each overtake.

*Maximise acceleration by using the best gear to conclude the manoeuvre in the shortest time.* Taking that gear in advance avoids the unwise and risky course of changing during the overtake. In the act of passing both hands are needed for steering; as the correct gear has been taken you should have ample reserve speed.

## PREPARATORY EYE-WORK
To analyse what might go wrong while overtaking you may need to move in left (cautiously; there might be a cyclist) to see past along the inside of the vehicle in front. To increase the gap between you usually helps in doing this. The gap principle applies even more to seeing round the offside and away up ahead, because it saves you having to pull out much if at all.

*Be unafraid of moving position relative to other traffic during this stage but be scared of forgetting to heed the mirror. Don't be hidebound by custom. Place your car on any safe inch of space available that helps provide the best view.*

Because this pre-view is a continuing process during which miles of road may be covered if you get few chances, it may only be possible at the first or any one check along the inside to decide, for example: "That will be okay. The road is clear and there is nothing to push this man out for the next six

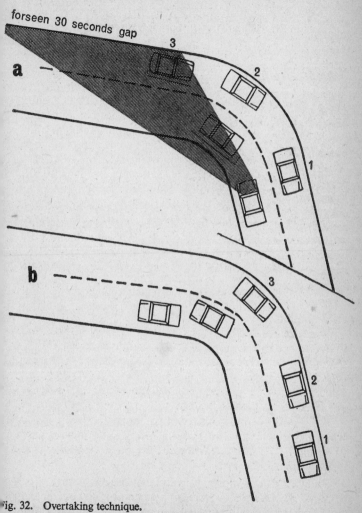

forseen 30 seconds gap

a

3

2

1

b

3

2

1

Fig. 32. Overtaking technique.

hundred yards—or, perhaps, all the way to a bend still a long way off—but I will have to re-check if, for other reasons, I haven't overtaken by then". Thus you inform yourself that, all other factors being in your favour, you could safely pass during this "time limit". You bear in mind once it expires you will have to re-check. Alternatively, your first peep may show there is no hope of passing, so you must wait.

## An Example of Preparation

You are following a car round a long sweeping left bend on a *wide* two-way road. You know or expect a straight stretch comes after the corner. Because of watching through and to the left of the car ahead for some time while approaching this sweeping bend you have observed that after the third car to come, there will be a gap of at least thirty seconds duration with nothing coming. This tees you up for gently nosing out to look round the offside of the car you want to pass at the moment the bend is straightening. That is, immediately the third car passes the other way. Fig. 32(a) shows your initial looking position and (b) your new position moved to during the pre-established safe moment.

From position (b) as the bend opens into the straight you need to be in gear ready to pass quickly, maximising safe use of the straight. If you can't go, drop back, in, if necessary and nothing is lost. Indeed you have gained another pre-view of what *is* coming and perhaps ascertained how soon you will find a gap, whereas, had you waited till after reaching the straight piece, you could easily have found it was too late to overtake safely before another hazard. The message is getting your view early, safely and ready to go or stay.

Sometimes in these circumstances you get a road-hog sitting on your tail. Try flashing your brake lights on and off as this may cure him; if not it is better to drop back and let such fools pass.

## Example of Preparation at Right Hand Curve

In anticipation of the road straightening after a right bend Fig. 33 shows positioning to see ahead and be at the ready. You tuck yourself in near the edge to gain the best view up the straight at the earliest moment. The technique demands watching lest something causes the lorry to pull out suddenly.

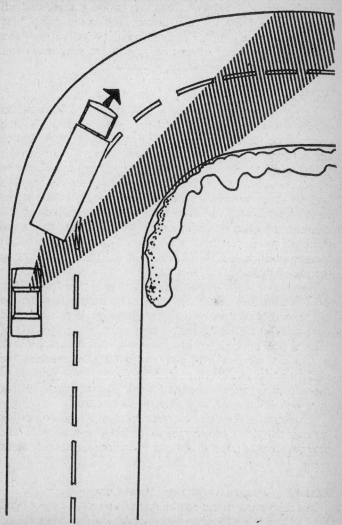

Fig. 33.  Preparation for passing.

It is not only concentrating on the road beyond the lorry but watching that the wagon itself does not change direction.

It is essentially early positioning to see which makes overtaking safer. If clear you can go quickly, before the chance becomes unsafe.

As with looking right and left at junctions it is the continuing sweeping view that counts. You must be sure no hidden vehicle can emerge and cut you off. Remember that there may be a dip in the road ahead with cars coming that you cannot see, for example.

### What Happens If He Pulls Out?

Even on straight roads and dual-carriageways you must be reasonably certain nothing will cause whatever you are overtaking to move out and rob you of your overtaking space or, more crudely, push you into a hedge! Causes might be rocks, a tree root, often a hidden cyclist, a puddle, wind, anything, *including the unbelievable happening*—cause of so many deaths.

EXPERIENCE IS OF NO VALUE IN UNPRECEDENTED CIRCUMSTANCES. YOU MUST BE WATCHING AND THINKING WHAT YOU ARE DOING WHILE DOING IT.

*Any car travelling behind another is liable to pull out to overtake.* You must hoot to warn such a driver of your impending pass. In case he is deaf, mirror blind or refuses to hear or if you have been catching up swiftly from a long way behind, drop to near his speed until certain he knows of your intention to pass.

Particularly on dual-carriageways and motorways drivers swing out without continuing reference or even a glance in their mirrors.

The reason many fast drivers have bad smashes is because they disobey the rule *that what matters is the difference between their speed and the speed of the car they are passing.* You must be faster to pass but *never so fast as not to have the control to stop if the person you are passing swings out or some catastrophe robs you of your passing area.* You must retain your "cocoon" of safety and swerve margin.

As you are passing your eyes range far and near. Just before you commit yourself to pass, glance at his front wheels which would give first warning of his swinging out.

This watching his front wheels (without dwelling on them, because you have other things to watch) is one of the great secrets of safety. Unless he skids, he can't come out if his wheels don't turn.

A hoot might be justified if someone did pull out while you were in the overtaking position but it dare not replace evasive action. Anger is foolish.

This wheel-watching is an even greater life-saver when an approaching vehicle is behaving dangerously. By keeping his wheels in the corner of your eye, you know if he is getting more or less dangerous to you, and act accordingly.

**WHAT TO DO IF THINGS GO WRONG WHEN YOU ARE COMMITTED TO AND NEARLY PAST A CAR** Advance planning is the answer. KEEP THE CAR PREPARED THEN YOU HARDLY NEED REACT.

### "Balance"

The faster the speed the more imperative to have the car balanced and going in a straight line. An emergency swerve might cause a skid. Braking and swerving could be worse, whereas braking in a straight line is relatively safer.

*From the moment you are committed to going on*, the secret is to aim the car straight to your SAFETY point of re-entry to the stream of traffic, i.e., to your side of the road.

At this stage there may be no danger. What matters is what may happen in the next split second. Approaching traffic may be coming quicker than you judged or an unruly member swings out to overtake towards you; or perhaps you will be overtaking on a clear stretch but with a bend looming near when a "fastard" sports rockets round straight at you or worse skids towards you. These are the sort of problems.

Fig. 34 shows the correct overtaking principle in plan. Rather than a haphazard round detour (the dotted path shows this "buppy" procedure) you ease out gently as far as point (A). Add speed in the process but don't over-accelerate and skid. From (A) *now going as hard as you safely can* keep straight as far as (B). You are still not committed. You are still straight and although hazardous, braking to drop behind would be possible. After (B) it is almost certain you must go on because attempting to drop back would be a greater risk. From (B)

101

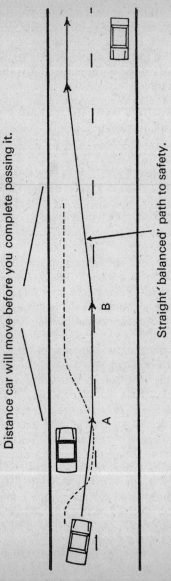

Distance car will move before you complete passing it.

Straight 'balanced' path to safety.

Fig. 34.  Passing principle.

*you must get balanced, going straight*, AIMED—allowing for
the distance the vehicle you are passing will travel in the time
(shown projected on Fig. 34)—*directly for your safety gap*.
Then:
  a) in the normal way you keep going hard till safely returned
     to your own side before steering back on course as shown.

### "Directional Confidence"

  b) should someone appear, even a "fastard", his confidence
     should remain intact. Your deliberate pointing in to the
     left (you can add left indicator) tells him you are *already*
     in command of the new situation. He has only to keep
     well left and judge whether to slow down.
*"WITH THE CAR PREPARED YOU YOURSELF
BARELY NEED TO REACT"*; to keep going as you are
(straight for safety) is usually enough and no panic need arise.

If you had been passing like an amateur you would have
probably had to swing violently to get out of the way, might
have skidded and caused a major accident. Frightened, the
oncomer could also blunder towards you instead of away and
skid in the attempt to get clear.

  c) in dire emergency on the other hand (e.g. two "fastards"
     appear, one *overtaking* the other!) you might *have* to
     brake towards your safety gap, keeping straight and
     balanced. Unfortunately the effect has to be to tem-
     porarily squeeze the car being passed. But the advantages
     in terms of life saving outweigh this and being already
     straight—poised if you like—*on your way to safety* the
     chances are you won't skid into the oncoming vehicle.

## TEXTBOOKS FRIGHTEN PEOPLE ABOUT
## CUTTING IN

Many learners are advised never to cut in till they can see the
*whole* of the overtaken car in the mirror. Incredible, for it
causes people to court peril. Even if you touch an overtaken
car, damage is likely to be slight; compare this with possible
multiple deaths disaster should you hit an approaching car.
The silly text books gloss over that!

Provided the car you pass doesn't have to slow there is no
reason for not cutting in as much as you want. It is amazing
how close you can go, particularly when your speed is well

above his. Glance (rapidly) over your shoulder and see the true facts.

Another aspect of being closer to safety than danger applies on three lane both-way roads. Irrational though it is you will notice that about 80% leave more room between themselves and what they are overtaking than between themselves and traffic passing the other way. Common sense dictates keeping nearer the vehicle you are passing.

The very advanced driver usually waits till he can get a clear pass, clear from *ANY* approaching vehicle.

## OVERTAKING PRINCIPLE FOR THREE LANE TWO-WAY ROADS

Custom, more than anything makes the rules. You give way to anyone approaching *already* in the centre lane.

You should be safe to overtake only if:

1) Nothing is coming (with slower traffic ahead of you over-taking in the centre lane, you can use the outer third lane. But you must be sure you have ample acceleration in hand that will enable you to regain your own side in safety, come what may).

2) Or, when only one vehicle approaches, and (a) you have had time to establish nothing follows it, (b) you are 100% certain no one you are passing might pull out forcing you into it.

3) Again, once you are sure members of the stream (or the single car) you are passing will not force you out, you should be safe even when several approach in their own left lane. PROVIDED *that none are close behind or catching up each other, thereby being likely to come out into the middle lane.*

My advice is, no matter how safe put headlights on and keep them on till back to your side.

In (3) above I discard the theory of avoiding being "the meat in the sandwich". I agree with the theory and usually practise it. But modern thick traffic conditions make application of the old principle impracticable every time although it can be combined with the newer "permissive" methods outlined. Use common sense, and extra care if speeds are high or conditions skiddy.

## FOLLOW MY LEADER OVERTAKING

Once one car moves out to pass, several more often tag on behind, hoping to get by as well. The only safe "tagging" rule is to keep well back from the leading overtaking car moving in or out as required to maintain a *continuous* view of the road ahead. Hoot each vehicle you pass as they probably won't expect a 2nd (or 3rd) car to be passing. Any approaching vehicle also sees YOU, a vital safety factor. You can watch whether the gap the man in front chooses will hold you all and still be big enough should he brake unpredictably. At all times strive to have a gap ready for emergency retreat. The secret is to keep options open for room to manoeuvre. If there aren't any, don't be there.

Many drivers are unaware of the above safety principles; imagine one such ass "glued" to your tail perhaps at speed while you are passing a convoy. Probably the mirror has warned you over the last miles that he is a fool. You must drive accordingly, rejecting any plan you may have had of keeping on passing till the last moment when oncoming traffic has all but arrived, and instead, move into an earlier gap. This leaves the madman on his own facing the oncoming traffic. He now has time to get out of the trouble of his own making. Your job is to look after everybody.

## THE WORLD OF DIFFERENCE BETWEEN AN ACCELERATING PASS AND PASSING WITH SPEED IN HAND

When you have to go all out to get by in time, the strain may break the engine or snap some vital part such as the accelerator cable. Caution insists it is better to have a spare safety margin of speed, otherwise never chance it.

When you arrive behind with speed in hand (a "flying" pass) ready to go ahead, the safety margin needed can be a little less while still ample, because you are not "straining" to get by.

Often by timing arrival at the overtaking point with expert (to an onlooker miraculous) judgement,—judgement developed from wary, early, experimental beginnings—you can keep speed going throughout for certain types of overtake. You thus benefit from the safety of speed in hand. For example, when you are arriving from well behind and have been able to sum up all the problems in readiness, you may have the opportunity.

1

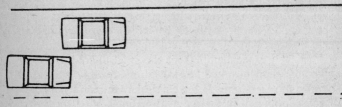

2

Fig. 35. Action! In emergency.

The trick is to reach the car you want to pass at the same instant as a gap develops in the oncoming traffic. This clear area lets you quickly, softly by.

With experience, relatively small gaps can be used safely. BUT, see the next section.

### Telling Someone In Front He Should Have The Chance To Pass First

When you catch up a queue held up by something slow you have to allow earlier arrivals a reasonable chance to pass first. Despite perhaps being ready to pass and lying out, if a car ahead shows determination to pass the problem, you are morally bound to *move in* behind him. This tells him via his mirror that you will wait for him.

If, however, he shows no sign of preparing to pass staying behind him yourself adds to the jam. Experienced positioning for vision and know-how may enable you to pass safely, when he won't or cannot. Go then, because every car out of the queue releases a space for the next arrival behind.

### "PRISON"

You are alongside passing a car which is forced out unexpectedly, for example as Fig. 35 shows, where a kiddy dashed out because her brother threw her ball on the road. *GIVE ROOM*

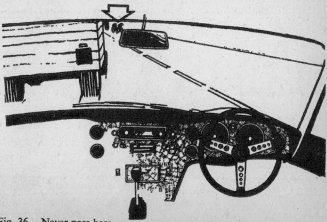

Fig. 36. Never pass here.

107

*to save life* is the priority action. Keep away from the car as much as you can and avoid shutting him in, so he can swing round the child. The split-second emergency may not give time for him to brake. Whether you try to stop or go on (do whichever is safer) is of secondary importance. The main thing is to give the car swerving space.

## THE RUSSIAN ROULETTE PASS

Despite the remainder of the road being clear only the foolish would try to pass the van ahead in Fig. 36 with approaching cycling children in the distance. The van need only wander slightly (driver looking at scenery etc.) and those kids are instantly at risk. They probably don't even see you because cyclists rarely look far ahead. Avoiding them is your supreme duty but you could so easily be unable to and the blame for the tragedy would rest on you.

# 6

# Bad Weather

## FOG

SPEED IN FOG MUST BE SUCH THAT YOU CAN STOP WITHIN THE DISTANCE YOU CAN STILL SEE.

Use *headlights*. Most sidelights are very small, and it is vital to be *seen* as well as to see. Dipped beam, day or night, is usually best. Fog lamps are useful but unless they are paired one either side, they should never be on without headlamps as well. A single light can be mistaken for a motor-bike and would be illegal at night. With a pair of fog lights on, remember your side lights, or you have nothing alight at the back.

In fog, maximum speed may be walking pace or less. Satisfy your conscience that your speed is safe. It takes *will power* to resist the temptation to tail someone who whizzes past. He may have superb eyes or lights but he is more probably an idiot.

Following another car and watching its brake lights may make things easier, if done from a respectable distance, but there is no excuse for mad close driving. Idiotic "tailing" causes countless pile-ups. The police should investigate all such accidents more than they do and prosecute bad drivers.

If following someone, switching off your headlamps may help, but this would be illegal at night because, except where street lamps exist 200 yards or less apart, it is obligatory to keep headlamps on unless you have a pair of foglamps, or one fog and one spot lamp, correctly fitted. (Lighting regulations can be checked in "Motoring Law A-Z" by J. L. THOMAS, an invaluable companion volume in this series). Make sure people coming do see *you*, however, by switching them on again briefly as necessary.

In fog range your eyes ahead, around—also *up* for traffic lights. Over concentrating on the edge lands you on crossroads before your mind registers. In misty fog, keeping the windows clean is half the battle. Use Wipers, and a cloth inside fre-

109

quently. Open your windows as fog dampens sound and the "air" keeps you awake! In desperate conditions you may see better by leaning out of the window but if it is that bad why risk your life when you can sleep in the car or stay at a hotel? Park well off the roadway, lights off (if you have to leave it on the side of the road—keep on your own side—side-lights on). Walk round to observe the safety of your parking position before leaving.

### Surprise Patches of Fog

Bewildering, especially at night, these patches are frightening at high speeds. Unfortunately the patches are most common on fast roads through open country. *Slow up at once—to a stop if necessary*. Don't speed on hoping the patch is brief. Re-acceleration later is better than dangerous "blind" driving. Remember the car behind (in the mirror) and try not to jam on your brakes too hard.

## SPITTING RAIN

Wipers used on a dry screen may damage it. The first sweeps to clear initial rain or spray from cars ahead may stir up dirt and mask vision.

### What To Do

a) Slow down, keeping left *till you can see again*.
b) Use the windscreen washer to clear the dirt quickly.
c) Stop the wipers while water builds up so the screen is "washed" when you next switch on.
d) *Be prepared* with a clean windscreen which gives the wipers a better chance.
e) Look at the road, not at the drops on the screen.
f) Always carry a clean rag or better, a leather, to use if needed.
g) For a misted rear screen a feathery mop on a four foot bamboo cane kept on the back seat enables you to lean round and wipe it from the driving seat while you wait at traffic lights etc.

## CLOUDBURSTS, TORRENTIAL RAIN

Almost all vision may be darkened or lost. While the worst is on, if you don't draw off the road and stop, use dipped headlights so as *to be seen*. If passing slower traffic use right indicator because these orange repeating lights seem to stick out like sore thumbs, pin-pointing you for oncoming traffic.

Disc brakes may become saturated wet and appear, on application, to have failed for a fleeting but frightening moment, before acting. Then they may come on quite fiercely. Initial sweeps by the brake pads on the discs have first to clear the excess water. The manufacturers generally advise occasional light pressure on the brake during such conditions to clear the bulk of the water. The importance of remembering, YES REMEMBERING, to do this cannot be over emphasised.

Another problem is saturation of any type of brake when deep flood water has been encountered. *YOU MUST DRY THE BRAKES IMMEDIATELY*, otherwise they can lose *all* power. While driving *at walking speed*, gently hold the brake on with the left foot, driving, as it were, against the brakes, till efficiency returns. *Always*, after going through any casual water, or a cloudburst, test brakes for loss of efficiency.

## OVERTAKING IN RAIN
Increase overtaking margins, I need hardly point out here— by a minimum of three times. Try also to be considerate by keeping well clear as you pass, and avoid lingering in that position from which your wheels directly spray the windscreens of those you have passed.

Next. . . .

## SUNSHINE
To cheer the reader feeling drenched!

### Dazzle In The Mirror
This is a sure sign that approaching drivers can hardly see you, so be ready to hoot and get out of the way. It is astonishing that many drivers still drive when they can't see for the sun.

### When Dazzled Yourself
The best plan is to squeeze the eyelids together seeing through narrow slits and continue slowly enough to be safe. Sun visors allow blinding shots of sunlight past them and also substantially mask the road ahead or to the side, but they can help a little when the sun is blinding.

Sun glasses or tinted windscreens have recently been proved in America to be a possible cause of accidents because parts of the eye may only be light sensitive to what the tint filters out. The research may be wrong but in my own experience any form of shade tends to make the eyes restful rather than alert which would seem to agree with these findings. Any dirt or finger marks on the windscreen make the glare inexcusably worse.

On bright days indicators and brake lights are less visible, and drivers get sleepy, so make allowances for them not seeing your signals—particularly people following if you are turning right off a fast road.

# 7
# *Night Driving*

## TWILIGHT OR DAWN, OR POOR LIGHT

Put on dipped headlights *early*, as dusk approaches, soon after you have put on your side lights. Contrary to popular belief this does not wear out your battery; leaving headlights off only increases danger. It is illegal to drive in darkness without headlights on unless street lamps exist two hundred yards or less apart. The half-light is a treacherous time because so many idiots, not having their lights on, are scarcely visible. Be extra careful when overtaking.

## IN TOWNS

Unless street lighting is excellent, dipped headlights or "Town" headlights of reduced brilliance are vital. You may be able to see without them, but you must *be seen*. People leaving side streets look briefly and pull out; they shouldn't but do. Their glance misses tiny sidelights especially if attention is attracted to a car *using headlights, further behind you.*

AND HEADLIGHTS SAVE PEDESTRIANS

### Helping People at Junctions

If a car waits in front of you to join a main road, switching off your headlights reduces glare for him and helps him see his way out. The front driver always needs his appropriate indicator to inform main road drivers and should have headlamps on. If a queue has formed and you are back marker, keep your indicator on to warn new arrivals behind who may then wish to position to filter to one side. Drivers queuing between the front and the back can keep indicators off to cut down glare, and for the same reason should avoid holding the footbrake on. Wet nights can be Hell when drivers ignore these simple considerations. The principles apply in many situations.

When following someone along a main road who begins to indicate for turning off, switch your headlights briefly off and on, and position appropriately, to tell you have the message.

## MORE TIPS FOR TOWNS AT NIGHT

1) Occasionally you will be leading a stream which meets a casual pedestrian or stalled vehicle. Because followers are less likely to see why you are stopping at night it is essential to stop as smoothly as possible and to leave a good space between you and the problem. This gives confidence to whoever is in your way; and if you should be bashed from behind, at least there is room for you to be shunted forward.

An early flash of your brake lights warns followers of approaching trouble. Only when absolutely necessary to save lives, stop so positioned that no one can get past you.

2) At dark junctions, looking right and left needs extra time to sweep across the shadow as distinct from the brightly headlighted patches. The eyes have to adjust. It is your *duty* to be on your guard for those rare but terrifying darkly clothed cyclists or kids coming, perhaps at speed.

### Following Other People

Dip so you don't dazzle. If dazzled yourself in the inside mirror offset it a fraction or buy an anti-dazzle one. Avoid the eyes dwelling on the wing mirrors. SLOW DOWN IF YOU CANNOT SEE.

### IN THE COUNTRY

Many are tempted to switch off headlamps when following on unlit country lanes.

DON'T because:

(a) It's illegal, (b) your width may be wrongly judged by oncomers, (c) your vision is gravely reduced, (d) the excuse that sidelights prevent dazzling the driver ahead is irrelevant because if dazzled he should go slower. To be considerate, avoid dazzling by dropping further behind.

An occasion for sidelights only, might be a crawling traffic queue but headlamps on when you move off.

### WHEN LEADING A TRAFFIC STREAM THROUGH COUNTRYSIDE

With nothing ahead and nothing coming high beam is *essential to see properly. Whenever someone comes—dip*, returning to high beam immediately he has passed if no others appear.

Prepare to dip in advance when you see light beams approaching a corner or the top of a hill.

If travelling fast towards a corner, give one or two brief up and dip flashes to warn on oncomer before he appears. (The same applies approaching brows of hills or other hazards.) BECAUSE: If the beams you have seen are from *two* cars, one overtaking the other, this alerts them to their folly. Human nature being as it is, people never expect you to be coming fast.

## THE PERMANENTLY DIPPED OR "DIPPY" DRIVER

Many lazy (or perhaps fearful) or inexperienced drivers don't bother with high beam at all—usually the slower drivers who are a hazard to those going faster. Safe overtaking opportunities are repeatedly lost because people behind can see only the length of the slower driver's dipped beam. Resulting delays and impatience lead to unnecessary death risks being taken. Please help faster drivers with high beam. Dip once they are past until they are well clear.

> THIS ACCIDENT-PREVENTING TIP IS SO IMPORTANT I CANNOT UNDERSTAND WHY IT HAS NOT LONG AGO BEEN PUT IN THE HIGHWAY CODE.

Please tell all your friends about it; the message needs to be spread!

## PASSING CYCLISTS OR SMALL OBSTRUCTIONS AT NIGHT

To help followers it is important briefly to give the right indicator in good time so that they have warning of somebody or something to be driven round, and can allow for it.

## SPEED IN THE DARK

IF YOU GO FASTER, IN THE PREVAILING ROAD CONDITIONS, THAN THE DISTANCE YOUR LIGHTS SHOW CLEAR AND SAFE, YOU'RE MAD!

Relate your speed to the area lit. Go more slowly on high beam than in daytime, and when dipped, more slowly still.

One pedestrian knocked flying because you never saw him in time, perhaps killed, saddens a whole family, not just the selfish driver. The reader may feel this is put too emotionally but I hope he will nevertheless check back his speed at night where necessary, after an honest self-appraisal. If you have been lucky in the past, remember that luck ends. Not everyone wears something white at night, especially not intoxicated pedestrians.

## DAZZLING

If dazzled (temporarily blinded) you must slow or stop till you can see. *Don't take risks or blame others*; you are responsible for your driving. Reduce dazzle by *concentrating on seeing your* side of the road. Do not allow the eyes to be "hypnotized" by approaching beams.

A *brief* up flash reminds an approaching driver to dip. But to deliberately dazzle back is childish, increasing danger. The other man's dipping apparatus might be broken.

Always dip *before* junctions or roundabouts because there frequently isn't time later.

On empty main roads flashing lights up and down, *even if there is no apparent approaching traffic*, announces your presence at hazards. *In the seconds you are dipped you see approaching light beams easily. In the seconds you are on full beam others see you.*

In traffic streams use your judgement to cut braking applications to a minimum. This saves brake-light glare for people following.

## OVERTAKING AT NIGHT

RULE ONE: NEVER OVERTAKE WITHOUT YOUR HEADLIGHTS ON.

If you are overtaking in the middle lane on three lane twoways—EVEN WHEN THERE ARE HIGH POWER SODIUM STREET LAMPS—*Keep your lights on.* Don't do it by holding on the flash switch (fitted to many cars) which brings on high beam. Put the normal switch on, dipped.

For ordinary overtaking with no oncoming traffic, a brief flash of your headlights warns that you are coming, but you leave switching on the high beam until you are almost along-side ready to pass.

## A Passing Headache

How do you pass a "Dippy Buppy" (see page 115) who slows more than necessary for every approaching car but speeds up whenever you are about to pass?

Lie well out when it is safe. Put on your high beam before you begin to overtake him. The temporary dazzle in his mirror may slow him down, but beware lest he is dazzled too much and swings out in front of you. You must be very careful of such selfish idiots. But this may prove your only method of seeing *far* enough ahead of him to pass safely.

## Extra Risks Overtaking at Night

Many motorists find it hard to judge distances at night. When you overtake on the open road it can sometimes happen that you are not quite ready to move back to your own side when a car approaches round the next corner. The danger is that an approaching driver may not realise at once that you are on his side. All he sees are two sets of headlamps with little speed differential or other guiding factor to tell by. Then when he realizes the true situation, he might panic. This makes matters worse.

To avoid this, you need to get quickly back to your own side —AND TO BE SEEN GETTING BACK. Use your left indicator. Worry less about cutting in than the possible head-on crash. The driver you are passing may expect you to cut in and be braking already. Strangely, drivers are less aggressive at night; he is less likely to accelerate to prevent you getting back, so a rapid glance over your shoulder may show you can move in sooner than you thought.

On the other hand, if on first seeing the danger, there was time and it was safe, you could have braked and fallen in behind.

## Signals for Night-Time Overtaking

Although it is a common practice, the use of right indicator when overtaking in daytime often has little value and can confuse other traffic. It may even be left "on!" At night a brief right wink during the early moving out stage makes it easier for following drivers (perhaps with poorer night eyes) to pick out just what you are doing ahead.

## ODD NIGHT-TIME TIPS

I recommend to faster drivers the very powerful long distance pencil-beam Quartz Iodine spot lights. It's a good idea to wire one into the high beam circuit to operate with high beam. This adds to normal headlight vision. Enough light penetrates further in front to pick out, and perhaps identify, any moving object way ahead. When travelling fast the early knowledge that some problem exists gives you time to assume the worst, brake, and get the car stably under control.

Quartz Iodine dipping headlights can be obtained to replace normal "sealed beam" units. Although expensive as compared to fitting a spotlight you get superb lighting.

## DIM LIGHTS

If headlights go dim: (1) Clean the outside glass. A few miles on mud spattered roads dulls lights more than you think! (2) Check fan/dynamo/alternator belt tension.

# 8

# *Motorway Driving*

## WHICH LANE

On three lane carriageways, whether you are travelling fast or not, the Highway Code rules you stay in lane 1, numbering from left, if 1 is full—2, and for passing only—3.

Sadly the rule is largely ignored. Frustration and accidents are caused because selfish "my speed", "my lane" drivers continually baulk faster traffic. Because a maximum speed limit exists is no reason for hogging the outside lane at that limit.

What happens so often is a mockery of our road building programme. Three lanes are provided but 85% of the traffic (lorries apart) is all choked "licking" bumper to bumper along the outside lane at precarious speed. On two lane motorways the problem is more acute. Crazy idiots keeping so close at high speeds are of course a cause of the devastating pile-ups which result.

When baulked you must NOT overtake on the inside, if you value your life and licence. If first behind the front road hog hoot "madly" and flash headlights which may be more effective. When second or a subsequent arrival behind, you have to wait your turn.

## DON'T FOLLOW DIRECTLY

A Very Advanced driver by instinct rigidly maintains his adequate "stopping and thinking gap" in such situations. Bearing in mind traffic behind and/or to his left another valuable trick he employs is moving slightly sideways relative to the line of the traffic, never sharply, so as to command the far ahead view. More often movement has to be towards the middle rather than out because of less room nearer the centre reservation; he thus protects himself from sudden unexpected jam-on braking which may ensnare less cautious members of the stream.

Not only on Motorways but always in traffic a wise driver avoids following in the wheel-tracks of those in front.

Remember what we said about keeping a "Cocoon" of safety and swerving area around you. If you are directly behind the vehicle in front, (a) you can't see well, (b) if he stops you may hit him, (c) if he hits someone you have little chance of swerving, and (d) if something heavy falls off his vehicle or is lying on the road the chances are you won't see it in time to miss it.

But if you are out of his track, even as little as 1 foot, you are able to see far further ahead and anticipate "trouble"; that extra foot, or preferably a bit more, gives you also the chance if safe, to swerve and miss an accident.

*This avoidance of following the man in front close, directly and blindly, is one of the great safety secrets.*

## MOTORWAY MIRRORS
A single careless check in the mirror may show a car without demonstrating its speed. Some reach 150 m.p.h. (lawlessly!) and can be on you in a breath. Therefore assess speed by several checks over a distance, before moving out to pass. Such a driver would be mad to pelt past at a great difference in speed as outlined on page 100, so let us pray the Very Advanced driver would not be guilty of this error, just as we hope he would never omit proper mirror checking.

## CHANGING LANES ON MOTORWAYS
Lane changing should be smooth and gradual in all normal circumstances, more so at faster speed to avoid unbalancing the car.

## RIGHT INDICATOR FOR OVERTAKING
Right indicator when changing to a faster lane is good as on a Motorway no confusion with making a turn can arise. Hold your finger on the control as reminder to cancel!

Left indicator when moving in to be passed? No! If you have room, move in, as this indicates perfectly that you have got the message.

## TELLING PASSING VANS AND LORRIES THEY ARE CLEAR
When a lorry or a medium van passes you, help it by flashing headlights once it is safe for it to pull in.

## SPEED EFFECTS

When the eyes and mind have long been focussing and concentrating far ahead for fast driving, consciousness of speed can disappear. 70 m.p.h. feels like 30 and this is *one of the most dangerous illusions in motoring*. It effects the inexperienced especially. Less experienced drivers should stop regularly at restaurants even if only for a 15 minute rest.

## OVERTAKING SNAG ON THE MOTORWAY

Suppose you are in lane 2 and continually passing slow traffic on the inner lane. Silly drivers often pull out from the inner lane regardless of you. Only an iron rule may now prevent a multiple smash. It is that unless you are certain that nothing is anywhere near catching up in the outer lane, *you don't swing out yourself*. Brake, let the fool out, and keep in your lane.

## DROWSINESS

If you are drowsy before reaching a stopping centre get into the inside lane, slow down and try these: open windows, pinch yourself, pop your head in and out of the window, breathe deeply, sing, whistle, shout, shake your head, slap your face, wriggle in your seat, etc., *but don't allow these to affect your driving*. If this does not work, stop on the hard shoulder to recover. If the police say they will charge you, tell them not to be silly. It is only fair to add I don't think they will because I have always found our motorised police sensible, but they may think you are drunk and ask you to take a breathalyser test.

## MOTORWAYS IN BAD WEATHER

Beware of fog patches; see page 110. The only sound advice is to keep off motorways if fog is heavy.

In wind grip the steering wheel firmly especially when going under and over bridges and the end of high banks etc. At such places the strength of the wind may change.

Never exceed 70 m.p.h. on wet; that is if you wish to reach your destination; (see page 127). Clear disc brakes of water, often. (See page 111). As you arrive to pass hefty transporters anticipate blinding spray for a few seconds. Have your windscreen washer full on in case this spray is muddy!

### When the Rain Stops

Usually one lane or a part of one dries first. If your speeds are in the 65–70 m.p.h. range, i.e. one of the fastest drivers on the motorway, getting onto the dry is tremendously important. Just the wheels on one side running on dry would be ten times safer than both on wet. So, taking account of mirror information, use the advantage of the dry area as much as possible.

### Snow—Black (Invisible) Ice

Chapter 10 on skidding discusses black ice, but snow drifts can also be frightening. Imagine a mass of snow is around but the motorway itself is clear to the tarmac (or has been ploughed clear). Traffic melts the bulk of any falling snow but at isolated points snowdrifts abruptly funnel say 3 traffic lanes into ONE NARROW ONE! There may be no warning of this hazard and at night the speed with which you can come on it is terrifying. It may be hours or days after the drift forms before it is fully cleared. The trouble is that one drift in a whole length of motorway is enough to land you in a pile up. Your "thinking and stopping gap" is the saving message.

## MOTORWAY ACCIDENTS

If you are involved in a smash and happily unhurt, remember that other traffic will pound relentlessly on. Drivers as a rule don't slow down; if space exists to squeeze through they will try, probably at 70 m.p.h. This is why minor incidents become fatal pile-ups.

If possible, without risk to the injured, get vehicles on to the hard shoulder preferably or central reservation. Flash brake lights continuously or operate simultaneous four-way indicators, if fitted. Make sure Police, ambulance and breakdown vehicle are telephoned at once from one of the free emergency phones provided every few hundred yards. If a red triangle is available put it out quickly (perhaps on the way to the phone) a good 440 yards back. At night take off dark jackets to reveal white shirts. Have someone flag people down several hundred yards back.

In the absence of medical knowledge cover any injured with clothing or rugs for warmth, but unless they are at risk from passing traffic don't attempt to move them. Check for breathing—you may have to attempt the kiss of life immediately.

Support the head if need be to ensure the person's windpipe is not choking because of his position. No drink should be given. Switch off the ignition of crashed vehicles and extinguish cigarettes to prevent fire.

## MOTORWAY TYRE PRESSURES
Most manufacturers recommend a few extra pounds for sustained high speeds; consult the handbook. The added pounds counteract flexing and heat, a tyre's worst enemy.

*The 70 m.p.h. limit is discussed in Chapter 11.*

# 9
# *Automatic Transmission*

## ONLY THE RIGHT FOOT

The right foot accelerates and also moves to the brake as required.

WHY:

a) The left foot braking method advocated by some people may confuse you in an emergency. b) You damage the transmission if the right foot rests slightly accelerating while the left brakes. The "right foot only" habit should prevent blipping the accelerator unintentionally in a traffic queue.

Don't laugh—it's easily done.

### Reverse With The Right Foot

Delicate reverse control is achieved with the engine ticking over simply by easing the right foot off the brake. Featherlight acceleration is added as required—using the right foot for braking. Hold the footbrake on while changing from *Drive* to *Reverse* or vice versa.

### Check Your Advanced (Correct) Moving Off Procedure

(1) Apply footbrake (right foot).

(2) Select *Drive*, release handbrake.

(3) *Hold* car with footbrake, check it is safe to go.

(4) If safe, right foot moves to accelerator.

### Advanced Hill Starting Off

Release handbrake instead of at (2) above, at (4) above, after *slight* acceleration makes the car strain to go.

### Traffic Queues

*Never* allow your handbrake below top efficiency. When queueing and stopped with the handbrake on select neutral to prevent "creep" against the handbrake.

124

**Changing Back From an Automatic to a Manual Drive Car**

Remember to put the clutch down when coming to rest. This is easily forgotten after many miles on automatic.

**Wet or Greasy Roads—Caution with Automatic "Kickdown"**

In automatic Drive beware of "kickdown" or forceful acceleration while cornering. An automatic change occurring (up or down) can cause a slight jerk, and temporary loss of power at a critical moment might result in a skid.

# IO

# *Skidding*

Probably 98% of skidding accidents arise from *lack of anticipation and knowledge of skid prevention*—resulting in dangerously excessive speeds relative to conditions. Only 2% may be skids which no reasonable driver could have expected.

Fortunately they are as easy to prevent as they are hard to correct. *Prevention is the life-saver* and it is prevention which you must, repeat must, learn.

## CAN YOU CONTROL SKIDS?

Sometimes corrective action eases a skid and enables an earlier return to control but because time and space to act are so often absent, escapes from severe skids without accident are usually due only to luck.

## THREE MAIN TYPES OF SKID

SKIDS WHEN BRAKING HARD

OVER-ACCELERATION SKIDS

THE DEADLY SIDESLIP SKID. (Where the whole car appears to slide bodily. It may be a front (or steering) wheel skid alone that gives this impression or ALL wheels, although apparently rolling forward at speed, may *drift*, skidding or sliding off the steered course; sometimes called a 4 wheel drift.)

Each type has similar causes:
a) Mechanical defect in the car
b) a Road cause
c) Human error

After a skid has happened you usually find a combination of (a) plus (c), (b) plus (c), or all three caused the trouble. The hardest to admit although strongest element 98 times out of 100 is (c) YOUR OWN STUPID FAULT.

## DEFINITION OF TERMS
### Locked Brakes

"Locking" means when a wheel or wheels *stop rolling*, momentum (weight x speed) thereafter carries the car along with that (or those) wheel(s) sliding.

### Aquaplaning

On wet roads, traction (road grip) gradually lessens as speed rises until the tyres, instead of gripping, are skulling on a film of water. Fig. 37 shows this, greatly magnified. It has been proved that the wheel actually stops revolving as it starts to aquaplane. The frightening thing is that once the front wheels aquaplane – ALL STEERING CONTROL VANISHES.

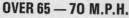

**OVER 65 — 70 M.P.H.**

Fig. 37.  Aquaplaning.

As a water ski-er will skim the surface at speed but sink when he stops, so cars "ski" and "sink". In *all types* of car (sports cars are no more immune than others) aquaplaning on a damp surface usually becomes serious about 65 to 70 m.p.h. but less if tyres or road surface are bad. LUCK SHOWS NO MERCY IF YOU EXCEED THIS BORDERLINE SPEED ON WET ROADS.

*65* to *70 m.p.h.* is the borderline *top* limit on wet roads, given the best tyres and a good road surface. But do not be fooled that such a speed will always be safe. On a straight open road empty of traffic with no cross-wind and no likelihood of being

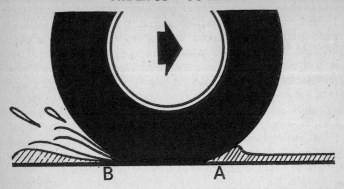

Fig. 38. How a tyre clears water.

forced to swerve or stop quickly, yes; but speed must be reduced for bends; if there is other traffic or any possibility of having to brake, no! Your "cocoon" of safety must be greatly enlarged. This usually means slower speeds. Your "stopping and thinking" gap has to be extended to counteract the possibility of *locked brake aquaplaning* explained below.

On wet roads up to 70 m.p.h. *good tread* can cope with almost unlimited road surface water by squelching it out behind and, depending on design, a certain amount is squeezed away to the sides. If there was no space for the water (AS WITH BALD TYRES) science would probably prove aquaplaning could commence about 30 m.p.h. As the famous Dunlop advertisements showed so well the area of tread which actually contacts the road at any given moment is only about the size of the sole of a man's shoe.

The tread works its "magic" by the revolving of the wheel bringing a constant fresh supply of "thirsty" tread. As each area of tread meets the road surface (A, Fig. 38) it *sucks* up the loose surface water. This the tread stores during the fraction of a second before again leaving the tarmac (B, Fig. 38) when it sprays it out behind.

### Locked Brake Aquaplaning

If you lock brakes on wet roads the tread is robbed of its mechanism for clearing away the water. The locked wheel(s) will tend to aquaplane until again allowed to rotate. They can continue to "ski" down to 10 m.p.h.—5 m.p.h. or less if stuck locked. What happens is the water, now a "torrent" because it can't get away, works like a continuous "wedge" into the angle between the tread (in front) and the road. This *lifts* the wheel into aquaplaning. While aquaplaning continues there is almost no effective stopping of the car and you have no steering control.

## SKIDS WHEN BRAKING HARD
Page 130 charts typical (a), (b), (c) causes, (see page 126) which can combine, starting these skids.

### Prevent These Hard Braking Skids
Keep the car in top mechanical condition. It is false economy and death-courting to use worn tyres. Brakes usually need adjustment each 3000 miles. Check air weekly.

At safe places check the treacherousness of any doubtful surfaces by testing. (See ROAD CAUSES in the chart, page 130). Start test braking at crawling speeds, increasing your experience with EXTREME caution, a little at a time, when roads are empty and no one could get involved. This is how advanced drivers are made!

The experienced maintain vigilance on all changing road surfaces. Any suspect surfaces are ALWAYS tested, speed being dropped till a test confirms it can safely be increased. If gradual icing is feared, for example at night, tests may be required every few minutes. You must know the condition of the surface at all times.

Test brakes under any extra load so that you appreciate the vast additional stopping distance required and the increased possibility of losing balance and control.

### Spotting A Mechanical Fault
Slow punctures can be detected by *heavier* steering or bumping noises. Wrongly adjusted brakes usually pull a car to one side, *progressively more so with rising speeds*.

It may be useless only to test a brake system at 30 m.p.h. It is often only at 65–70 on dry roads (test gingerly to start with) that a fault is sufficiently magnified to be noticeable.

# SKIDS WHEN BRAKING HARD

Wheel(s) lock(s) up. Car slides forward, may lose sideways control and begin to spin round or all steering may be lost if (on a wet road) Locked Brake (front wheel) Aquaplaning occurs. Results are exaggerated if the steering is in lock (e.g. turning for a bend), or if braking on a corner or adverse camber and on downhills, or when extra loads are carried.

*Likely*

## CONTRIBUTORY CAUSES

### (a) MECHANICAL DEFECTS

Treadless tyre(s). Soft or over-inflated tyres. Slow puncture. Front wheels (or rear) not having tyres of matching tread pattern, *condition* or type (e.g. radials mixed with cross ply). Over-loading. Lopsided load. Wrongly adjusted brakes. Poor suspension-particularly shock absorbers (which dampen up and down reaction of the springs at bumps). Other more technical defects causing "locking".

### (b) ROAD CAUSES

Wet surface (raining or not). Slippery surface (oil etc.). Mixed surfaces having different anti-skid properties. Cobbles shiny, or wet. Loose surfaces (gravel, wet leaves, mud etc). Uneven surface. Black (invisible) ice or "freezing" rain, Slush, Ice/Snow.

### (c) HUMAN ERRORS

Sudden stabbed instead of progressive braking. Excessive braking pressure by driver. Human error in not making allowances for (a) and/or (b) or having sufficient regard for exaggerating factors (see above) is the chief reason for these skids. BY KNOWLEDGE ANTICIPATE. Advanced drivers almost never skid unwittingly. They know the terror and drive to avoid skids.

I have made a brake test at 45 m.p.h. and the brakes appeared perfect; yet, in the same conditions, when absolutely safe to do so, I have found the car is swung to one or other side by a test at 70. This was the only early indication the brakes needed repair; if the test had not revealed the fault, any emergency braking might have ended fatally.

You must always know the exact condition of your brake power.

---

ON WET, INCREASE YOUR "STOPPING AND THINKING" GAP THREE TIMES MINIMUM; ON ICE, TENFOLD MAY NOT BE ENOUGH. A vehicle can skid for 200 or more yards.

---

### How to Deal with Hard Braking Skids

(1) Steer straight or as straight as possible instantly. Turned steering encourages brake locking and tends to throw you off course.

In the fastest possible stop, wheels at no time lock but are held at the point of locking throughout. The retarding effect utterly depends on tyre grip against the surface. The constant supply of fresh tread maintained by keeping the wheel rolling is what matters.

Directly a wheel locks, one small pad of tread has all the work to do and no hope of retarding as effectively. This tiny area of tread abruptly finds itself scraping along the abrasive surface leaving a trail of skid rubber. It heats rapidly, and may even start to melt. WORSE on wet roads, it may simply aquaplane instead, (see page 127).

To apply precisely the hardest possible pedal pressure that will still not quite lock the brakes needs more than genius.

(2) So in practice, IN EMERGENCY you press firmly (if need, rapidly increasing the pressure till quite hard) to the point where a wheel does lock, INSTANTLY EASING A FRACTION when this happens, so as to unlock. *Equally instantaneously*, for a locked wheel generally releases within a split second of your easing, *back on with resolute pressure to the lock point* ready to ease—only *ease* note—coming back with firm pressure the same as before instantly it unlocks again. By repeating this procedure you strive towards the ideal that

131

will stop you fastest—holding the brakes on the point of locking throughout.

Partly because speed is dropping all the time the tyre tread can cope with progressively harsher pedal pressures without locking. What I am saying is that your pedal push squeezing the brake linings against the wheel drums or discs can increase as speed drops to a halt.

Your repeated ON . . . EASE—AND INSTANTLY ON AGAIN process, to ensure your brake is as near as possible to the locking point at every stage, automatically makes certain you apply this mounting pressure as a stop is reached.

If you foolishly lock the brakes for too long the car may begin to spin. Once she starts to turn—your warning—the dramatic abruptness with which you can find yourself spinning more, going backwards, or crashed, is terrifying.

As (1) above tells, steer straight if humanly possible. Directional stability returns mostly during the seconds brake pressure is eased but you must drive to straighten immediately and continue to correct as necessary.

When you feel the back beginning to slide to one side or the other or in popular jargon, "to overtake the front" you must steer the SAME way; as the motto has it steer "into the skid", left if the back slides left, right if right; you must ease the brakes too, to help stop the back sliding.

### An Extremely Rare Occurrence

You are desperately trying to stop but control disappears from the front of the car. No response comes from the steering; no amount of easing the brake seems to unlock the front wheels. You may not have noticed greasiness or ice as the cause or on wet roads, it could be locked brake aquaplaning (see page 128). Until this situation rights itself there is usually little you can do except keep trying. However, a sharp hard-on handbrake jab sometimes induces the back to slide or in some way slightly alters the balance of the car and steering control returns. Instant handbrake release then allows you to steer to safety and braking can be gingerly resumed.

### So Far We Have Looked Mainly at Theory

What happens when you are faced with "piling" into stopped traffic?

Inattentive anticipation has landed you (an advanced motorist?) in so extreme an emergency that there is neither time nor sufficient distance left in which to stop.

*Answers*

1) If there is a clear pavement, or room to the right *without head-on danger*, steer for it! (Note: mirror knowledge might reject this move). You might have to ease braking substantially initially to get the steering response required.

2) Hoot! Stopped traffic might realise and be able to move forward; anyway it warns them to expect you and they may avert neck damage by holding their hands round the back of their heads.

Going back to (1) above, the advanced driver is continually planning during traffic conditions where sudden stops are likely where his escape routes could be in the event. His mind is probably subconsciously working on this and if a stop happens, as a passenger you would suddenly notice that he has "manufactured" a stopping or clearing distance out of "nothing". Although you may feel he sometimes follows traffic closer than you think he should he always has an alternative "lined up".

**An Amazing Skid**

A friend, driving through a town at 35 m.p.h. was suddenly confronted by a long lorry which shot across his bows from a

Fig. 39. Avoiding a direct killer smash.

133

walled side road shown by Fig. 39. He realised he had no chance of stopping in a straight line.

To avoid a direct killer smash he therefore steered right, deliberately swinging on to the arc shown by the arrows which lengthened his space for stopping. This more than compensated for the more difficult braking "on the turn". From about half way round his wheels actually locked and the car slid bodily sideways towards the lorry.

He finished up parallel to the side of the lorry, only 2″ away, but even had he hit it the accident would have been unlikely to injure as he had by then slowed so much and as the whole side of the car was ready to take the load of the crash.

While the car slid bodily towards the lorry in the last few seconds with all wheels locked the edges of the tyres probably did the last bit of sideways stopping by "scraping" dragging across the road surface.

A world authority on skidding said the action taken was probably the only possible one to save a crash. Unfortunately *such evasive action can not always be taken* because of other traffic.

## MORE ABOUT SURFACES
Please also refer to the chart on page 130.

### Wet
*On wet surfaces, brake locking starts more easily and earlier than on dry.* Required stopping distances are dramatically increased. CUT SPEED GENERALLY BY 1/3rd AT LEAST; also MULTIPLY YOUR "STOPPING GAP" THREE TIMES OR MORE.

### Slippery Surface (Grease, Oil)
On an oily surface, even featherlight braking may still lock the wheels, because the tyres cannot grip against the surface; they just slide. Fortunately lightness in the steering or a slight over-acceleration skid may warn you grease exists in advance of the need to brake. Accept any such warning as a MAJOR alert.

After a shower or as rain commences, oil drops and general dust left by traffic appear to mix and rapidly spread into wide areas of "ice-rink" conditions. Only heavy rain seems to wash

134

the oiliness away. Damp patches on otherwise dry roads are particular traps for the unwary, partly because one comes upon them at faster speeds.

### Loose Surface (Gravel, Wet Leaves, Mud, etc.)

Your tyres grip the leaves, mud, etc., but these slide over the road; take the warning as no less grave for being obvious.

### Black (Invisible) Ice ... The Big Killer

In populated areas weight of traffic and the effect of gritting and salting usually keep most of the important roads usable. Overnight frost is quickly melted to a damp surface. This is fine (except in open places where ice may remain for longer) until the late afternoon or perhaps later when, as traffic diminishes and the temperature again falls, the "black" ice begins to form again. How can you tell just when and where the damp turns to ice?

*By ear.* Through a slightly open window you can hear the characteristic hiss of the tyres on a damp or wet surface. On ice all is quiet, deathly silent. The contrast is your *immediate warning.*

Like grease, ice may also identify itself by lightness of the steering—or a slight unexpected tail waggle—a general uncertain feeling in the way the car responds to the controls.

*Expect such signs in wintry conditions.* Take the hint if you see lorry or other professional drivers going slowly, or if ice is forming on parked cars. Much over 15 m.p.h. or 20 on black ice is extremely risky. "Freezing rain" as weather men call it is very similar and in minutes the road can turn so glassy that driving becomes practically impossible.

### Snow or Snow with Ice on Top

From the braking point of view snow is nasty; iced over as well it may be diabolical. For normal stopping use gentle braking.

If even gentle braking locks the brakes, drop down the gears until she grinds to a halt in 1st, using engine compression control. But note that the slight jerk as you let in the clutch with each lower gear may lock the driving wheels should you not match road to engine speed fairly accurately. (See how to double de-clutch, page 32).

## OVER-ACCELERATION SKIDS

One or both driving wheels spin or fail to grip the road to move the car. There may be loss of sideways control at the driving end as well. (Most cars have rear wheel drive but some, like the Mini, have front wheel drive.)

*Likely*

### CONTRIBUTARY CAUSES

| (a) MECHANICAL DEFECTS | (b) ROAD CAUSES | (c) HUMAN ERRORS |
|---|---|---|
| Soft or over-inflated tyres, Slow puncture. Treadless tyres on one or both driving wheels. Overloading or lopsided loading. Other obscure defect. | Wet surface. Slippery surface (grease, oil, etc.). Mixed surfaces having different anti-skid properties. Cobbles shiny, or wet. Black ice/Freezing rain. Snow/Ice on top of snow. Adverse camber may accentuate loss of sideways control. | Ferocious acceleration in lower gears or jerky acceleration. As above when on a bend or corner makes a skid more likely. Using too low a gear. Human error in allowing for (a) and (b) lets these skids happen. BY KNOWLEDGE ANTICIPATE; BY CAUTION, PREVENT. |

So slippery can conditions become that even at walking speed just turning the steering for a corner is sufficient for the wheels to lock and slide. When this happens you go straight on, not round!

*At speeds under* 10 *m.p.h.* on snow you can sometimes use this fact she will go straight on with the wheels turned, to help stop. While continuing to brake, swing rapidly on to full lock so that your tyre edges "scrape" at the snow. You will find the car still goes straight to start with. When it begins to turn, as it will, switch fast over to the other lock. Depending how compactly the snow has been beaten down this technique may be a help.

If you must drive in such lethal conditions another thing you should do is to make use, where it is *in your favour*, of the camber of the road. While no one can guarantee to control a skidding vehicle, the very advanced can, *by studying the road camber, at least, usually, skid in a safer direction.*

It is the driver who gets on to the wrong camber at a border-line speed who is a menace—even getting an inch onto the wrong camber can throw you off-balance into an accident skid.

When snow and ice come, get on to an isolated road and study the immense effect road camber has on skidding. You will discover, in safety, what quite extraordinary things camber can do to you, and how to use it correctly for safety where you can.

Other tips for stopping on snow are: Get onto fresh snow near the edge if you can; the tyres bite better. In real danger bumping the edge or aiming for a snow drift could be better than careering down a steep hill. At hills always stop or drop to snail speed at the *top* to assess the situation before descending. It's too late half way down. Depending on traffic on severely cambered roads (high in the middle, falling away to the edges) it pays to keep near to the middle so that braking or sliding doesn't take you into the gutter.

I have known a hill become so slippery that when I tried to stop at the top before going down I could not! She slid on and on, although quite slowly. I therefore slipped the gear into *reverse* and gently began to spin the driving wheels backwards.

Like "magic" this measurably checked my speed, already gathering with the steepness of the hill. Although too much reverse wheel spin started to turn the car I was able to control speed sufficiently to reach the bottom safely. Flashing my headlights warned people waiting at the bottom that I could scarcely stop. Fortunately they understood.

## OVER-ACCELERATION SKIDS

This category has similar (a), (b), (c) causes which are charted on page 136.

Control of these acceleration "wheelspin" skids as they are often termed is normally simple IF THEIR CAUSE IS QUICKLY GRASPED. The skids happen when starting from rest and, with more ferocious results, if accelerating too harshly from one speed to a higher speed. Judgement of surfaces and controlled acceleration are the chief weapons of prevention.

### Starting From Rest

A surface may be so slippery that moving off is impossible without some wheelspin. The secret is to use the HIGHEST gear that will just take the car away without stalling and to almost stall in the process. This minimises wheelspin.

On snow you must get this right first time or the wheel very quickly becomes dug in. You must also keep the steering straight until away or you make it harder. Advanced drivers watch where they stop on snow, knowing how easily cars stick. Every trick of timing is employed to avoid complete stops on uphills or against the camber. Care is taken in parking, etc., so as to be able to get away later. Getting out is thought hard about before going in! "Fools rush in . . ."

### More on Snow

Short uphills are tackled with a cautious build-up of speed (after waiting for any drivers ahead to clear) to keep going in the highest gear; longer hills are best tackled from the bottom in the gear that will get you to the top and beyond because the chances are if you have to change, wheelspin might defeat further progress. If you have to change down, do so with confidence, quickly and try not to lose speed.

If the driving wheels end of the car slides sideways in getting away it will be because wheelspin is excessive. Directly you reduce wheelspin by easing acceleration (just enough will do) steering control should return.

Spinning the wheels on snow wears tread away almost as fast as snow to further deter you from the practice! But if a wheel digs itself in, and you have tried all the tricks helpful bystanders urge, try turning off the engine, leaving in neutral and simply pushing the car out of the hole. It works! The same applies on mud. Often the secret is to reverse into a better position to start away from. It is wise to carry a spade.

**Go Up It In Reverse**

Occasionally, especially in the country, the surface is so slippery you cannot get up a hill at all, even a slight incline. If there is a grass verge and you can get your wheels on to virgin snow, the problem is frequently solved. There may, however, be instances when the only way to get up is to reverse up. With a back-wheel drive vehicle this may work when forward fails. Provided it is safe it is worth a try.

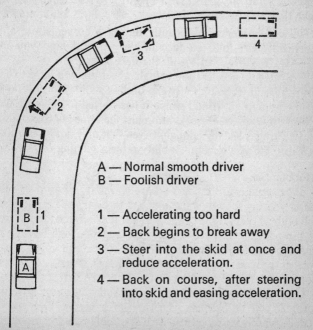

A — Normal smooth driver
B — Foolish driver

1 — Accelerating too hard
2 — Back begins to break away
3 — Steer into the skid at once and reduce acceleration.
4 — Back on course, after steering into skid and easing acceleration.

Fig. 40.  When the back "hangs out" – rear wheel drive.

## OVER-ACCELERATION SKIDS AT FASTER SPEEDS

Just as experienced drivers test dodgy surfaces for braking, they learn to respect slippery surfaces that may induce over-acceleration skids at corners. In icy or wet weather keeping in top gear where possible helps to avoid these (though this is not of course an excuse for excessive speeds!) In the lower gears ferocious acceleration from any speed may start wheelspin. On "banana skin" conditions even cautious gradual acceleration may provoke trouble.

Readers may have heard the expression "hang the back out" on corners. This describes what often happens in a wheelspin skid with rear wheel drive; the back of the car slides outwards off the corner as if Fig. 40. (Unfortunately sometimes greatly assisted by bad camber, see Fig. 41.) With front wheel drive the front end may behave similarly though not usually so suddenly or so much.

*To nip these slides in the bud, as to stop any wheelspin, simply reduce acceleration—*NOT COMPLETELY—*sufficient only to stop the wheelspin.*

To cut acceleration abruptly during a corner could affect drastically the total balance of the car and land you in a DEADLY SLIDESLIP skid, the next category.

As you ease acceleration to halt wheelspin you have to steer into the skid (the same way the back is sliding) to prevent the car spinning right round which it has started to do. With front wheel drive you ease acceleration just the same but to straighten the steering is usually enough. (Even that may not be essential.)

From the very second stability returns (sliding or wheelspin

Bad camber increases the chance of an over-acceleration skid, and its severity.

Fig. 41. Danger of adverse camber.

dies) steer for where you want to go again and you must gently increase acceleration to "set" the car back on course. This is done without returning to the previous level of acceleration, which was too high, and is ESSENTIAL to recover from such a skid.

## SLIDESLIP SKIDS
The chart on page 142 shows likely contributory causes of these.

These skids are so terrifying and DEADLY, I urge you to accept that prevention is the only safeguard. Within seconds of a skid starting cars can spin, roll, hit walls or jump precipices, and as easily at 60 m.p.h. as at 17 m.p.h. on ice or wet.

### Inexplicably, The Car Ahead Suddenly Spins Off a STRAIGHT Road
I have witnessed this several times. Sheer excess speed causes it. For example a fool goes 40 on black ice (while others keep under 15 m.p.h.); some minor incident causes him to touch the brake or alter steering, and whoops! he'll be lucky not to break his neck in the nearest ditch.

Or, if you overdo speed on wet (remember the border line top speed on page 127) and the front wheels aquaplane, then the slightest bump, gust of wind, steering movement, braking, or perhaps one or both front wheels hitting a flood puddle could twist the car sideways in a trice—too fast to correct. (Even at normal speeds hold the steering tight at puddles).

### Cornering Too Fast
Before discussing how to try and avert or reduce disaster when once in the clutches of such a nightmare skid, I'll explore the most usual cause:

Any car tends towards driving straight and only "wants" to corner if steered. As speed rises *straight on momentum* (weight x speed) and centrifugal force progressively oppose efforts to steer round corners. When speed gets too high they beat the steering and you go straight on. It follows that slight bends can be taken relatively fast compared with tight corners, which require substantial steering.

From the chart, page 142, you can see other factors vitally affect cornering too. Your safety depends on whether the tyres maintain their sideways grip. Mechanical defects may

141

# THE DEADLY DANGEROUS SIDESLIP SKID

The whole car appears to slide bodily. A front (or steering) wheel skid can give this impression or *all* wheels, although apparently rolling forward at speed, may *drift*, *skidding* or sliding off steered course; sometimes called a 4 wheel drift. These skids happen if a car is simply cornered *too fast*, or as a result of hard braking (usually on a corner), or they may be induced if an excessively sharp steering movement is applied, and held, *suddenly*. If steering lock is deliberately and *suddenly* over-applied at any stage during a fast corner the front tyres can slide, even on a dry road. See page 144.

*Likely*

## CONTRIBUTORY CAUSES

### (a) MECHANICAL DEFECTS

Treadless tyre(s), slow punctures. Soft or over-inflated tyre(s). Poor springs or faulty shock absorbers. (These lessen the up and down reaction of the spring after a bump). Front (or back) wheels not having tyres of matched tread pattern, *condition* or *type*. Different types of tyres wrongly fitted to same car. Overload or unbalanced load.

### (b) ROAD CAUSES

Wet surface (rain). Slippery surface (oil etc.). Mixed surfaces having different anti-skid properties, Surprise wet patches on generally dry roads. Wind. Flood water. Loose surface (wet leaves, gravel, mud etc.). Black ice/"freezing rain". Snow/ice on top of snow. *Adverse camber alone or combined with above.*

### (c) HUMAN ERRORS

Excessive speed for conditions. (Even going straight). Cornering too fast for conditions. Human error in making allowances for (a) and/or (b) is the tragic fault that results in these skids. BY KNOWLEDGE ANTICIPATE; BY CAUTION PREVENT.

upset this grip; any slipperiness on the road would too, perhaps encouraged by adverse camber. *Always watch your camber.*

If you reach a corner too fast relative to conditions your steering attempts are bound to be beaten to some extent. DON'T IMAGINE IT WON'T HAPPEN TO YOU.

When you really overdo speed into a corner the car skids approximately straight on, helplessly, appearing to slide bodily off the far side of the corner because initial steering effort first turns her partly sideways.

### So How Can The Fastest Cornering At The Limit Of Safety Be Achieved?

The ability to feel a car's "balance" "through the seat of the pants" and maintain it, perhaps best defines the difference between the skilled driver and the amateur. Clues as to what this means can be gleaned from the following experiment:

Find a *deserted* straight and *dry* dual carriageway with two lanes and adjust to about 40 m.p.h.

From the left lane "throw" the car over to the right lane with a quick steering movement. Almost a twitch on the wheel is enough without altering the position of the hands, instantly straightening and holding rock steady in the new lane.

Notice how much of the car's weight seems to plunge towards the two outside wheels; you can feel those tyres digging into the tarmac. Now "throw" the car back across to the left lane (mirror permitting) and feel the same effect the other way. By this deliberate steering you can set the weight of the car to some extent where you want it.

When cornering, centrifugal force and straight on momentum try to throw the car out, off the corner. The most important counteracting force is the grip which the two *outside* tyres manage to hold. The weight is lifted from the inner side of the car so these inner wheels only exert a slight helpful grip.

THE MORE EQUALLY THE OUTER TWO WHEELS SHARE THE WORK OF OPPOSING CENTRIFUGAL FORCE AND STRAIGHT-ON MOMENTUM, THE BETTER. If excessive weight lands on the *front* outer wheel it cannot help but succumb sooner and slide. This is what happens when you brake excessively at a corner.

By cautiously extending experience, you learn just how confidently the weight can be thrown deliberately on to the outside wheels, when a corner is reached, with the tyres still able to accept this onslaught and not lose grip (at the speed and surface conditions prevailing). *Begin experiments at lower cornering speeds than you have been used to. Certainly do not start to learn on wet roads, or anything more slippery. It would be easy to throw yourself too hard and into a slide.*

You can acquire the knack of angling towards a corner (within the confines of safe road space available) so that *when you reach it* you can throw the weight gently in the most equal possible way on to the outer wheels to thus achieve the best balance of the car for going round. (Note that at left hand bends you dare not risk anything if traffic is, or may be coming.)

I say "*gently*" throw the weight. You are setting the weight by a deliberate steering movement. At high speeds or on wet it can happen that too sharp a steering "twitch" makes the front tyres slide immediately. Instead of setting the weight nicely and steering the car round the bend, the front wheels slide and you go straight on. *Reduce* the steering lock at once to stop this sliding. Should your steering movement cause the back of the car to slide out although the front went were you wanted it you must steer "into" this new rear wheel skid momentarily to regain stability. Either of these dangers is possible if you jerk the steering too hard relative to your speed and the sharpness of the corner. DON'T DO IT.

### The Limit of Adhesion

The single most important factor about the limit of adhesion (any conditions) is not where it is or its measurement; it is the *way in which you approach it*. I have discussed keeping a cocoon of safety around your car (page 95). Here it is more than anywhere applicable. Never approach the limit without having room outside your (intended) line through a bend to recover should you overstep. And secondly ensure that any overstepping you do is of a kind from which it is easy to recover.

There is a saying "Slow in, Fast out" at corners and here comes part II of fastest safe cornering.

### "Slow In, Fast Out"

When you accelerate you will notice the front of the car lifts, and the back beds down. You make use of this fact.

144

By steady re-acceleration from half way round the corner—in practice probably from a little earlier—you counteract the natural tendency for most of the weight to act towards the front outer wheel. Acceleration lifts some of it off the front and transfers it on to the back.

Because knowledge of the principles and increasing experience may encourage you to corner faster, I MUST WARN YOU AGAINST BEING CLEVER AT BENDS, ESPECIALLY BLIND ONES. The old maxim DO NOT DRIVE FASTER THAN WOULD ALLOW YOU TO STOP WITHOUT SKIDDING IN THE DISTANCE YOU CAN SEE TO BE CLEAR must still be rigidly applied. Traffic may be halted round the bend.

The process described above is sometimes termed as "setting the car up for the corner".

Use of these principles is of greater importance the faster one tries to corner. There is, naturally, A REAL LIMIT to what is possible no matter how skilled one is. Controlled use of the methods is enough for normal cornering at normal speeds. Remember some professional racing drivers have been killed trying to take corners too fast on ordinary roads, so don't take risks.

## PREVENTING SIDESLIP SKIDS
YOU MUST SLOW SUFFICIENTLY ON APPROACHING A CORNER SO THAT WHEN YOU REACH IT YOU CAN MAINTAIN BALANCE GOING ROUND AND KEEP WITHIN THE LIMITS OF TYRE SIDEWAYS GRIP.

At normal speeds one eases the accelerator approaching a corner and arrives on "trailing throttle" (foot not completely off the pedal) well inside steering limits, ready for re-accelerating. Faster drivers often approach a corner using brakes.

### The Technique of Braking Into a Corner
Under firm braking the nose of the car dives, bringing more weight on to the front wheels and lifting it off the back ones. This makes turning at the same time very dangerous because balance is lost and too much weight is thrown on to the outside

front wheel. ALL HEAVY BRAKING MUST THEREFORE BE DONE WHILE STILL ON THE STRAIGHT, AND BEFORE BEGINNING TO TURN.

If you have created your own crisis by slowing down too late your best hope will probably be *to brake resolutely to the last inch you dare to keep straight,* steering to get you round beginning simultaneously with lifting your foot off the brake. This ensures that the weight gets evenly distributed to the outside wheels; steering throws it outwards; lifting off the brake lets the front rise again and stops too much weight going to the front outside wheel. Slight re-acceleration *straight-a-way* even trailing throttle—should, if anything can, maintain balance till you steer out of trouble. You have had a fright; avoid them!

This will almost certainly be better than braking so harshly in panic before and into the corner that you find yourself in a locked brake slide, or a spin, ending up out of control, "all-over-the-place".

Normal braking, approaching a corner with good timing, and steady accelerating out of the corner is excellent practice for establishing confidence. Cornering on SIDESLIP, the terror of all, will be discussed after a few more precautionary tips.

### Allowing Room For Error

If cornering near the limit of adhesion is your pet vice, go back to smoking; it's safer! Seriously, the only thing is to position to allow the maximum possible space for sliding around.

The photo on the outside of the book shows the author taking a roundabout for straight on, fast, but safely. Having slowed enough approaching the roundabout, and seeing the in-between road to his left clear, he takes the rest of the roundabout accelerating firmly, but—as you can tell—a slight acceleration skid of the rear wheels occurred. His safety margin had allowed for this possibility knowing it would only be a skid of a few inches as the road was *dry.*

Note the bodywork of the Lotus dipped evenly towards the outside wheels and the steering exhibiting what is called "opposite lock". (The steering is turned the other way to the direction of the car, i.e., into the skid, See page 140.)

The message of this photo is that the car is tucked in close to

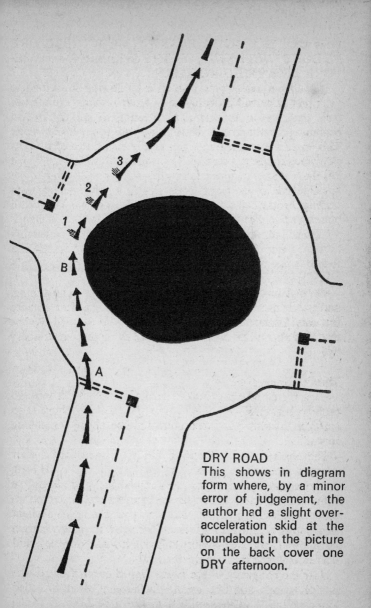

DRY ROAD
This shows in diagram form where, by a minor error of judgement, the author had a slight over-acceleration skid at the roundabout in the picture on the back cover one DRY afternoon.

Fig. 42. High speed technique for a dry roundabout.

the roundabout leaving maximum yards to slide on to before danger could arise. If the tail "hangs out" 2 feet before gripping that's twelve times safety margin if you have twenty-four feet to play with.

Fig. 42 shows his fast entry line to the same roundabout. Eye drill has established there will be no traffic on the roundabout. The weight is thrown *gently*, well within grip limits, *towards* the roundabout first as he almost clips the left hand entry kerb, so maximising safe sliding distance between himself and the roundabout edge, while balance is being established between A and B (Fig. 42). Within a trice of balance going in left, being confirmed and resumption of slight re-acceleration to maintain it, he can and does transfer the weight to where he now wants it by steering right again, round the roundabout.

Only from that stage does he get himself tucked in close. He probably travels straight—"balanced"—between A and B. In the whole process he strives to minimise the amount of turning needed at all.

At no stage in this lightning roundabout technique dare one risk a speed that could result, from being too fast, in any type of skid—especially a front wheel or SIDE-SLIP skid. Nor is it wise to leave braking as you reach the entry so late that any HARD BRAKING type skid could arise. In fig. 42, an over-acceleration skid did occur at 1 but instant reduction of acceleration curtailed it by 2, with full control returning just after 3.

### When You Haven't Room to Allow Space for Error

Keep tucked close to the left on left hand curves or well over and watching the camber on right hand ones, and GO SLOWER. I could list many safety examples. If there is traffic or limited vision, GO SLOWER STILL. The Good Lord usually looks after those who take no undue risks.

### Eliminating SIDESLIP Even on "Ice-Rink" Roads

Sideslip risk can be eliminated even on the worst conditions by *slowing down enough*, *and far earlier than usual before a corner*, to a safe speed so the whole bend is negotiable on slight acceleration. Any over-acceleration skid should be ended by reducing acceleration.

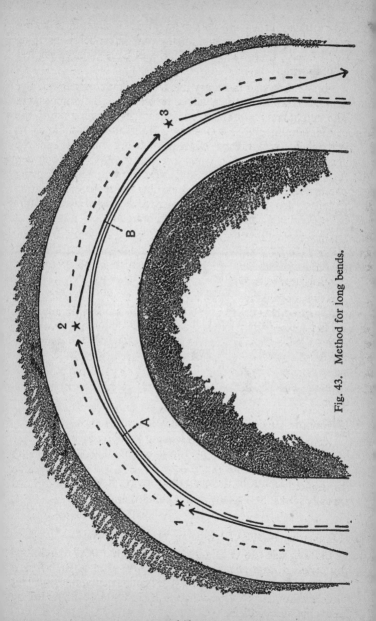

Fig. 43. Method for long bends.

## Sweeping Wide Bends

A long wide bend need not be driven as a continuous curve although this is normal and an acceptable method.

ON DRY ROADS ONLY, faster drivers may wish to learn the following technique.

Nearly all the road width is required so it is not practical for slower drivers owing to danger from fast traffic ready to overtake. The need for space also limits full safe use of the technique to dual carriageways. However the *principle* may be partially applied on very wide two-way bends provided you keep within the limits of your own side and well out of the way of any approaching traffic. In describing the technique below I have assumed that you as a driver would have checked for certain in the mirror that no-one behind could be endangered.

You assess the bend as having a number of steering "points". Fig. 43, 1, 2, and 3 shows how these "points" might be spaced on a typical long curve in this instance working on your own side of a double white line. Between each "point" you hold the steering on a curved course towards the next, but the radius of each of these curves will be less than the radius would have been for one continuous curve. (The continuous curve is also shown dotted in Fig. 43.)

The effect is to straighten the bend. A slight curve may require only one steering "point" to "straighten" it while a sharp bend could need three or even four "points".

Under "fastest cornering", from page 143, I discussed "setting" the weight of the car by a steering movement. At each steering "point" in this technique you a) "set" the weight, and b) put yourself onto the curved course required to the next "point". *You must remember the limitations to "setting" the weight in this way which were discussed.*

Ideally the path of the car between "points" will shave the inside edge of the bend or of the line as shown at A and B in Fig. 43 but this is less important than making certain that your "points" are well away from the outside edge. Your safety margin will only be as large as *you* make it.

Here are the safety reasons for this method of cornering:

a) Apart from the "points" where you set the weight you are not cornering so acutely. The car is better balanced for any *unexpected emergency*.

b) The deliberate setting of the weight at each "point" gives

150

you a more exact *feel* of how well she is balanced. It confirms you are safely within the limit of adhesion.

By contrast the feeling of grip (or lack of it) loses definition if a long bend is driven as a continuous curve.

## LAST RESORTS

Imagine for one of the reasons in the foregoing pages, or somehow, you have got yourself into a ghastly SIDESLIP. Suddenly the front is dancing to her own tune and nothing you try is making any difference, or she (the car) is going sideways, even perhaps practically backwards. Keep your wits. Never yield to panic.

Assuming you haven't already hit something, a quick action may save you but you have to realise that going through a hedge may be more Christian than managing to correct a skid but landing yourself in a head-on crash, killing innocent as well as guilty. Circumstances will flash such realities into your mind and help you to judge.

The instinct of self-preservation coupled with acquired understanding of the importance of balance may be most useful. You'll be thankful if you *have allowed room* for mistakes.

### Catching a SIDESLIP in its Early Stages

Steering to straighten the front wheels into line or nearer into line with the back ones, and getting them to roll again if they were locked, are usually the first essentials if you act early enough. (Turning the steering beyond straight—i.e. to "opposite lock"—could make matters worse.)

Now straight, but probably going in a dangerous direction, braking may be next priority before steering to try to clear a crash. Alternatively, within a trice of even a vague feeling of grip returning, you may be forced to try and steer to miss something. This will again tend to throw the weight onto only two wheels but skill and luck could take you out of trouble.

The supreme quality in driving is having nerves of steel; the greatest folly is to take advantage of having them. If, however, you are mentally strong and alert you may realise that your slide is subsiding and a way out would be to accelerate and "hang the back out" at the same time steering into the newly created over-acceleration skid. You would probably only get away with this on dry road in a powerful car.

151

If a sideslip is mild but threatening to get worse, as it might on a long and wet corner at high speed with bad camber aggravating the trouble, holding the accelerator dead on the exact road speed (neither accelerating nor allowing engine braking) may precariously maintain balance. Rather like walking a tight-rope; a slip and you are off the road. The hope would be that the sliding off the corner would subside before the wheels touched the edge or hit an oncoming vehicle. Drop acceleration just a fraction too much and the slide can take charge; accelerate a razor's edge more than it needs and you get an over-acceleration skid, and the car may spin before *you can steer into it. To come out of a serious skid in traffic alive needs luck.* Beware of any who offer to show you how to do it. Even if they paid me £50 an hour I would not accompany them!

## Too Late! A SIDESLIP Has Turned You Almost, or Completely Round, or the Car is Spinning Further Round than just Backwards

Don't "freeze" in terror. Most spins subside within 180 degrees and the car rolls on backwards. Getting the steering straight helps this happen. Quick wits in putting the brakes on once she is running back may save you from smashing something solid unnecessarily. If you have not been driving on the wrong camber this kind of skid may possibly be less deadly than some, though terrifying.

Having come to rest, move the car out of danger if possible, or abandon ship and comfort passengers. Don't sit to be hit! Don't be a Buppy.

## Let Skidding Fools Miss You

Suppose you see a fastard coming towards you at a bend so fast, he is likely to skid into your road space. It is here that the Buppies are sorted out from the Very Advanced. The former sail on to probable death, hypnotised, as is a rabbit by a weasel, by the super speed of the approaching car.

The experienced have estimated where the fool will skid and in the half or quarter second of thinking time for keeping alive, have either slowed, so the chap will skid in front, or speeded up, so he will skid behind or more likely, slowed and got as far away from the maniac as possible to give "all the time in the world" to avoid the hurtling mass of death as it skids past.

As you see him coming helplessly at you, you can often so angle your car that he only hits your tail-end. Or, so that your two cars will only "bounce" softly off one another by making sure you hit parallel, whole side length, to whole side length. With your car controlled you can act.

## UNDERSTEER AND OVERSTEER

Most cars are designed to *under*steer. In normal (non skidding) cornering the car runs, instead of on the precise arc the steering would theoretically determine, slightly wider—a fraction outside the curve steered. All the wheels "slip" by a tiny amount— invisible to the naked eye—further out than the curve to which they are pointing and thus the circle radius which the vehicle as a whole follows is fractionally greater than the precise circle steered.

In designing a car to *under*steer the makers ensure that the amount by which the front tyres "slip" is always slightly more than the back tyres. Thus at ultimate cornering adhesion speeds the front tyres should slide first—the increasing "slip" as the limit of cornering grip is reached comes to the "breakaway" point earlier at the front.

If a car *over*steers on the other hand the rear wheels will tend to break away first; the breakaway itself being so swift and complete few drivers can cope. For these and more technical reasons it has become accepted that an *under*steering car is safest for most drivers.

*The difference (or lack of it) between front and rear tyre pressures as recommended by car manufacturers may be as much as 20 pounds per square inch* AND IS SCIENTIFICALLY CALCULATED TO ENSURE SLIGHT UNDERSTEER. Keep to the instructions or you may find yourself with dangerous *over*steer. Incorrect pressures are illegal.

# *II*

# *Very Fast Driving*

**THE OVERALL SPEED LIMIT**

For the disciplined driver in the right car, speeds above 100 m.p.h. at times, *even on our crowded roads,* may be safer than 40 m.p.h. for the wrong man in any old car who lacks road-sense.

From my observations many "follow like sheep". Buppies, (explained in Chapter 1) who previously kept below 50/60 m.p.h. are tempted up to 70 by the limit itself, regardless of car or experience.

When it comes to the understanding of psychology, the Ministry of Transport are like suckling babes without even the instinct of self preservation. They lack the wit to see that when they say "O.K. up to 70 m.p.h." the Buppies will step on it for all they are worth.

Just as the £50 travel allowance brought out innumerable travellers *because* they had not realised you *could* go abroad for £50 so the 70 m.p.h. causes the Buppies to feel this is safe or it would not be legal.

A few who went 75 m.p.h. may have dropped the 5 m.p.h. while others who always went faster have now crept back to their 90 to 100 m.p.h. habits, but ever more watchful for police.

This silly British law deters them little and for them I include tips about high speeds because not to would fail the cause of safety. And there are no limits in many other lands.

Rather than accept that drivers have largely ignored the limit, as can be seen in day to day traffic, the Ministry of Transport seems to prefer to insist on its having some magic safety property. After the endless reports and statistics which heralded its introduction—the results—in truth somewhat doubtful—seem to be set down to confuse and to defend the original contention, so the limit stays.

I suspect the Ministry is obsessed with a notion that if they could restrict speed enough, accidents would fall for which the great Ministry God would be praised. The welter of limits, restrictions and advisory rules almost defeats imagination.

A future Minister may feel that keeping idiotic speed limits helps to win votes. This I doubt. It is going too fast in the wrong conditions that kills while speed in the right conditions can often save lives.

The need is for police to catch the few maniacs who endanger life in the 30 m.p.h. limits, as much, in fact more, than for exceeding 70.

What the statisticians, emotionally overcharged spokesmen and do-gooders conveniently ignore is that PRICE works more for safety than speed limits. The all-encompassing nature of an overall limit seethes with folly and unfairness. *The price of insurance*, by contrast, levied at rates kept down by the force of competition and conversely forced upwards by high premiums related to the type of risk, automatically provides a balanced and fair deterrent. The premium charged is related to number of accidents, age, experience etc., and is a strong deterrent to dangerous speeds.

This is not the perfect answer if such exists but the insurance cost has for years restrained youth (or inexperience) and bad driving with ever heftier premiums. The same chopper (or even refusal to insure) has applied to extra powerful cars, all note, *without state intervention.*

The overall limit tends to duplicate this deterrent function carried nobly by the insurance world; worse, it is harrassing the motorist, deflecting his concentration from the road ahead to his mirrors and down side turnings etc., searching for hidden police cars and radar traps.

Thousands of smashes must result or indirectly result from this universal diversion of attention—universal at least to almost every driver.

*I favour throwing out the overall speed limit.* I happen to believe that for motorways **and** some very good roads and the more alert drivers, in daylight, 90/100 m.p.h. (on dry only) is as fast as the eyes and brain can cope and still provide quick enough reactions should the approaching scene suddenly forecast risk. The condensed—"tunnelled"—eyesight limitations of most ordinary roads enforce this fact. *But I would not set any limit.*

I also believe that to exceed 70 m.p.h. *at night*—EVER—

no matter how fabulous car or lights—is LUNACY. No "night-eyes" can spear the darkness safely over 70. But to have the same 70 limit in wet or dry, day or night, brings the law into ridicule and tempts buppies to carry on sleeping up to it.

## SELF DISCIPLINE

Sad that so few possess this quality, imperative at speed. Any fool can accelerate; the problem is stopping.

Driving fast safely is a skill achieved only by practice. Even attention to the right principles and care are not enough to permit a novice to suddenly step "on the gas". Knowledge from books alone, or hearsay, is useless until experience over years and hundreds of thousands of miles is added.

Self discipline includes the honesty to accept exactly how slow your reactions are and if they, or concentration, are being affected by illness, tiredness or anger. Self discipline needs the ability to adjust your fastest speeds downwards to compensate for any personal defects. Human nature hates to admit such failings which makes such discipline a test of conscience and character. At 75 your reactions are slower than at 30 years old.

The chief qualifications for fast driving are wisdom and experience. It would not be exaggerating to insist on 200,000 miles as a minimum for learning. Till then one is a babe in road-craft and know-how. Many of our "young bloods" die because they refuse to concede this. Seventeen to twenty-four are the "insurance-proved" dangerous years; the years when most people, on account of their age, cannot have the experience behind them. There is no substitute for it.

By attacking the overall speed limit I may have hidden what I mean about very fast driving. What I stress centres rather on maintaining high average speeds than on whether the speed happens to be above or below any arbitrary figure or limit.

On winding or busy roads very fast driving could be under 45 m.p.h. all the time. The highest speed compatible with safety and ever changing to match the differing conditions, is the secret of the fast driver who gets safely home, and never scares others.

## "DESIGNED-IN" SAFETY

Family cars in good order can be driven briskly; certain high performance versions based on saloon models are fairly safe driven fast; a number of sports machines are mechanically identical to their saloon counterparts so must be classed as equivalent only to them.

For VERY FAST driving one must assume the car as one having "designed-in" safety—a car built throughout for speed. Among the few British makers of such delightful and safe machines rank such names as AC, Aston-Martin, Jaguar, Jensen and Lotus.

Lotus deserve great credit for giving such wonderful value with their outstanding Elite, Elan, Europa and Seven models. The Lotus record in racing, as World Constructors' Champions (Formula 1) six times, in 1963, 1965, 1968, 1970, 1972 and 1973, is unique. "Critics" have classed the Elans for example, as "Ultimates" in handling by comments (from memory) such as these:

". . . Spectacular controllability providing a new measure against which all future cars must be judged. . . . Through traffic—Squirtability. . . . Perhaps the only cars in which averaging 69 m.p.h. without once exceeding 70 would be possible. . . ."

Such remarks are not exaggerations.

I have owned two Elans in succession in recent years and I can vouch for this. It is because I love these cars that I write the chronicle of fast driving knowledge around the Lotus.

## Mechanical Condition

Tremendous stresses are created by fast driving. Only a few makes of car are *worthy of speed and safe at speed*.

Such cars are designed to work under constant pressure, snappy cornering, powerful accelerating and braking—but these machines *must be kept mechanically tip-top* to perform safely.

This applies to any car and speed but the rigours of long distance or regular speedy driving necessitate a perfect instant response from all controls and surging engine power. The condition of steering, brakes, tyres, lights and engine must ever be 100% for your own and the public safety.

## Some of the Fabulous Attributes of the Lotus Elan

Features worth comment include the safety resulting from reserves of power on tap, (for overtaking and for "setting" balance during corners when taken fast), finger tip steering even at 110 m.p.h., braking that stops in less distance from 110 than the average car manages from 80 m.p.h. In theory figures might prove this technically impossible but the experience for a driver in trying to emergency stop an ordinary car from its flat out "shaking" 80 m.p.h. is so frightening, compared to the smooth deceleration of the Lotus from 110 m.p.h. plus, few would possess sufficient courage to brake hard enough in a family car to do it.

The family car begins to shudder much above 70 anyway, but all who have had to emergency brake at over 75 m.p.h. know the sickening feeling of uncontrollability which often results.

The Lotus driver lives without such hair-raising experiences.

More spectacular perhaps is the clam-like grip at corners, giving the impression of an unseen hand laying a cast iron grip on the road surface.

The Lotus can *safely* whirl round curves at 70 which would find a saloon squealing at 40 m.p.h.

Another impressive feature is the suspension which lets the Lotus wheels ripple across all the bumps but at the same time eliminates almost all up and down movement of the bodywork. (Pitching, especially on corners, undermines front tyre grip.)

Lotus acceleration is breath-taking. Only those who have driven such cars as the Elan can believe they exist. I've taken middle-aged people for a run which they have described as the thrill of their lives. One of the best (and safest) things to show your friend is the standing start. If this is properly done (on a dry day of course) it is astounding but only exhibit it to people with sound stomachs! Some over 60 might not stand the excitement.

I did a 495 mile trip with a lady of 57 who normally is dead-beat after 200 but the comfort and feeling of safety and relaxation were such that she was almost as fresh on arrival as when she left home—as I was myself.


## THE DRAWBACKS OF SPEED

So extreme is the difference in "drive-ability" between cars such as the Lotus and mass produced models it is not surprising few drivers have much conception of their astonishing potential. In a fast car the way in which bunches of traffic can become slight problems instead of major bugbears has to be experienced to be believed.

Fast driving in these cars requires treating all you pass *as if they had no idea you were there*. Even conscientious mirror users may not appreciate how suddenly they can be caught up. The overtaking possibilities in many situations appear in a different perspective to the Lotus driver.

Even if *aware* of your presence many find it unbelievable you could pass *when* you do. (The most likely motorists to spot your arrival behind are other fast drivers in above average machines. Experience of speed driving has raised their reaction speeds, anticipation and motoring sensitivity to a high degree of excellence.)

As explained on page 100 the difference between your speed on overtaking and that of the person to be passed is crucial. A major advantage of the Lotus is the ease with which cruising speed, having been cut to the safe differential for passing, can be almost at once resumed.

A family car could need half-a-mile to build up the required speed and its driver may be loth to cut it in consequence. He is tempted, having at last got where he can pass, to take a chance *even* if he is not quite sure he will have enough time. This is a deadly dangerous cause of crashes.

Not so the Lotus man; once he sees all is clear, he can gather up his acceleration and shoot past into the safe gap. No fear for him that the family car he is passing may contain a "nasty bit of work" who will "race" him and try to stop him getting past—because by the time the horrible driver (and there are a few) has decided to close up, it is too late. The Lotus has gone.

One drawback, for it is not always allowed for by others, is the capability of the Lotus to corner while approaching "unseen" traffic FASTER THAN THAT TRAFFIC CONCEIVABLY EXPECTS. Therefore although *you*, may delight in cornering at speeds verging on the incredible, because you could scare someone into a panic—YOU MUST NOT. It is different where you can see through the corner.

On blind bends only madmen risk running into stopped traffic, a crash or an overtaking vehicle approaching round the corner. It usually takes two speed maniacs to kill each other!

In cornering at speeds wisely related to vision, fast drivers usually cover the brake during the critical seconds when any danger could be revealed. They always aim to position to allow for straight line braking should any emergency arise in the unfolding scene.

Slight cutting of speed during a dangerous stage by braking may improve the technique, because on seeing any emergency the car is already partly in braking equilibrium.

Becoming airborne over hump-backs can happen in fast driving, though one should not go so fast; don't brake—you would land on locked wheels; and don't turn the steering—most dangerous.

## ILLUSIONS OF SECURITY IN FAST CARS

There is a limit to what even cars like the Lotus can do. Fix that firmly in your mind, and especially for your first 100,000 miles keep on remembering it and realize that, no matter how perfect, a machine can only do certain things. But more. No matter how good the machine, it is driven by an imperfect person, you. You, the master, must make due allowance for all your weaknesses, perhaps night eyesight or slower-than-average reactions.

To become a master driver first master yourself. Self-control and self-knowledge are the rules for very advanced driving.

In your early ownership of a fast car be content to drive it *far below its capacity*. These are learning days; in *safe conditions*, experiment with how the car can accelerate, steer and brake. Get acquainted with when it will skid or not corner safely. Learn the car's reactions in dry, damp or icy conditions on clear roads so that your mind will be attuned to the limitations. For the first 25,000 miles drive no faster than you would a family car. Learn carefully over many months so that you come to know what you can do.

Learning is THINKING, until experience and knowledge can make an "instinctive" reaction.

One danger is to imagine—particularly on wet—that speed is lower than it is. I find Lotus speeds invariably higher on the same wet corners where I drive several miles per hour slower in an ordinary car.

A study of the skidding chapter shows the need for keeping the right balance of initial speed, steering and acceleration during cornering. Cornering near the limit of adhesion at the higher speeds possible in such fast cars requires greater sensitivity to judge balance, and an error—not appreciating how near the limit you are—is therefore more dangerous.

Reasons are these:

a) recovery action if tyre grip breaks away is harder in proportion to higher speed.

b) in slow old cars even heavy-footed acceleration as you leave a corner may not cause an over-acceleration skid whereas a touch on the throttle at the same place and speed could in the Elan. With surging power under your toe you dare not waggle it carelessly.

## A GLIMPSE AT THE FAST DRIVING EXPERT

Because of his car's direct steering action most bends don't require altering hand position from 10 to 2. The wheel turns, the arms bend but the hands remain. He can have no doubt (the amount off centre of his arms tells him sub-consciously) how much steering lock he has applied at any moment. This is very useful in getting the feel of what is happening to the steering wheels.

When cornering at speed he may push with his left foot against the floor beside the pedals to lock himself into the driving seat and stop his bottom sliding.

To a passenger he appears almost constantly to alternate between light or firm braking—never more nor less than required—and resumption of swift acceleration. Even on motorways he rarely holds one speed long. There is constant action or reaction; the slightest doubt ahead is met with instant speed reduction. The thought that it may be nothing serious is rejected along with wait-and-see thoughts, for without immediate braking control being gathered he knows it could be too late. Very advanced drivers try to be ready *before* emergencies.

His observation seems miraculous and the religious way he slows for hazards MORE than almost anyone else—despite going faster than they would dream of when it is safe—appears out of keeping with such fast general driving.

At high speed one notices his concentration is on "shall I have to brake" and when he does he always begins unexpectedly early. He understands braking distances at top speed are far greater than any eye could judge within feet. The good fast driver keeps an immense safety margin in hand.

*His speed is usually only high when the road is empty*. He then uses the middle of it frequently, to give extra manoeuverability should a tyre burst etc.

*On clear, see through curves* he takes maximum advantage of any camber and may "cut" or "straighten" these corners when safe. But he would never "cut" a corner if it meant putting the car on the wrong side of the road inches from a blind gateway or lane. There's too much danger of someone nosing out, or swinging out of it, not expecting him to be coming on the "wrong" side.

# 12

# Crashes and Extraordinary Circumstances

From the torrent of increasing statistics one could devote a lifetime to researching accident causes. Typically of Whitehall almost no attention has centred on which smashes to aim for, if there is choice, when an accident is inevitable. Lets bring some horse sense into the problem.

Among the killer crashes that should be avoided at practically any cost to safeguard life I would list the worst as these:

1. Being hit by a train on a level crossing.
2. Knocking cyclists or motor cyclists flying.
3. Hitting pedestrians.
4. Hitting or being hit side on (the doors of a car are usually the weakest point).
5. Head-on into another moving vehicle.
6. Head-on into solid objects such as trees, parked vehicles, brick walls etc.
7. Skids resulting in hitting lamp posts etc., which can cut sideways through passenger or driver's compartment.

Individual differences of speed, confines of space, etc., might place these in a different order, but the list probably covers the most fatal types of accident.

## SAFETY BELTS

The purpose of belts is to prevent the fragile human body being thrown against anything hard or out of the car when it is stopped abruptly. Even emergency stops cause passengers, unless expecting it, to be thrown forward, when a vulnerable part such as the skull may be cracked against metal making death likely. While a little evidence exists against belts, they do appear to reduce risks of death and severe injuries and on balance are worth using, especially in bad weather. Loose belts may be dangerous although over-tightening is unnecessary.

## POINTS TO REMEMBER IF YOU HAVE A CRASH

Theoretically you need only stop if *damage* or *injury* has been caused to another person, vehicle or animal outside your vehicle; with the abominable modern tendency for people to make untrue and preposterous allegations of blame, even if you are guiltless you could be well advised to go on your way quickly and quietly before being accused of dangerous this or careless that.

But if there has been damage or injury you MUST STOP by law.

Then you must give your name and address, and the vehicle owner's as well (if different) and the vehicle's registration number to anyone having reasonable grounds for requiring them. If anyone has been injured you also have to produce your certificate of insurance for anyone with reasonable grounds to see it at the time. This is all the law demands of you.

The Highway Code advice says just this but it is frequently misinterpreted. *Only if you are unable to or do not wish to comply with the above do you have to report the accident to the Police.*

Then you have to do so as soon as practicable and anyway within 24 hours, and you may have to produce your certificate of insurance for the Police.

Knowing the legal requirements yourself, don't forget to obtain all the information you are entitled to, and more if you can get it, and *note it all down*. Witnesses often almost fall over themselves in their rush to leave the scene uninvolved, but do try and persuade them to give you their names and addresses and perhaps a statement of what they saw.

Remember, as a witnessing driver hastens off, you might be lucky and trace him through the Licensing Authority by his number. If any office or house windows overlook the scene, enquiry might find someone who saw the accident.

Although most witnesses try to vanish, there are usually one or two people, probably fellow motorists who will offer evidence. If you are innocent, a good witness (unless in a fatal accident) will rarely be called to Court. A guilty party hardly ever goes to Court if you have a couple of witnesses, and you can explain this to them.

The essential need for the witness is to save your insurance companies cost and your own "no claims record" and driving reputation.

If you are not guilty I urge you to give priority to getting witnesses and evidence.

Finding out who insures the other driver may help; on the other hand if he finds out your company and later spins some tale of lies, as is common, you can find yourself in a tricky position. All measurements, photographs or other factual evidence you can gather will probably help in event of any legal entanglement, and it is wise to sketch the scene while it is clear in your mind. Measure distances from the edge of the road, skid marks etc., and record them on the drawings you make.

You must not admit blame even if you are at fault. To say nothing on the subject may be a condition of your insurance policy.

*Even if you believe a crash was not your fault*, IF PEOPLE ARE INJURED, *you naturally have a human duty to see that the best is done for them before any consideration of the points raised above. See page 122 for advice.*

## RUNAWAY CAR (BRAKE FAILURE)
Hold steering wheel tight, continually "pump" the brake pedal —you may regain some braking—bump kerbs, graze walls, etc. Also, "smash" gears down—straight to 2nd, then 1st, hoot again and again in quick succession and put on headlights to warn. The handbrake may be more help than you can feel (although it may cause the car to spin); miss anything, rather than hit something solid. If you are not on a downhill, taking lowers gears (plus horn and lights) may suffice to stop you before disaster.

## BURST TYRES AND PUNCTURES
With a puncture you get warnings, e.g. heavy steering, bumpier ride and loss of normal "balance".

A burst (blow out) is rare. If it happens, you may hear the hiss, or (if you have hit something) anticipate the burst but possibly your only warning is *sudden* reduced control as the car swerves. Up to 30 m.p.h. a burst is not usually serious and even at a higher speed a *rear-wheel* burst may not cause an accident.

Over 40 m.p.h. a front wheel burst can be grave. Act. Never panic. If your *front* tyres are good and you *avoid* hitting kerbs or objects, you may never have one.

Bursts are "instantaneous". Grip the steering tightly. Use strength to try and steer past danger. Aim to slow and stop with some braking but you may have to avoid further un-balancing the car by only braking lightly. As the car swerves you may have to battle with the steering to avoid hitting any-thing or going over a precipice!

If the car can be allowed to slow as it loses momentum that is best but if the "burst" is not quite instantaneous you may be able to brake before the tyre is flat. Most bursts are prob-ably caused by hitting kerbs or something like that, unless the tyre is already in bad shape. If you are a fast driver examine tyres for visible damage or any "bulging" every week.

## ACCELERATOR STICKS FULL ON

Action: de-clutch (press it down) at once. Switch off engine and into neutral quickly, before the engine "revs" its head off. Pull up as soon as safely possible.

## RUNNING OUT OF PETROL OR BLOCKAGE

The danger is that this may happen as you are passing someone and using maximum acceleration. The engine splutters and fails.

Action: keep cool and stop carefully. Wise people don't drive on an empty tank; they check the gauge as they get into the car, *as of habit*, to decide if petrol is needed.

## ENGINE STALLS (STOPS)

Action: as a life-saver, if about to be hit (e.g. on a level crossing) but can't start, move on the starter in 1st gear. The battery should take you to nearby safety. If it does not and a train is going to hit you don't just sit there! (People do.)

## BREAKDOWNS ON FAST ROADS

If you break down on a busy road, don't wait to be hit. Try and push the car or "drive" it on the starter on to the verge if there is one. Get someone to alert traffic if any danger. Open the boot lid and lean the spare wheel or back seat etc. against the rear bumper. This is a universally recognised breakdown signal. If you have an accident "triangle", use it. Above all get the vehicle on to a safe place.

# 13

# *Brief Notes on European Driving*

Most of the following applies throughout the continent although minor differences exist in the various countries.

**HEADLAMPS**
Your lamps must dip to the *right*. The easiest way is to buy the excellent clip-on yellow covers available for a few shillings. The light beams are "bent" to the right through the yellow lenses.

**INSURANCE**
Make sure your policy is right before leaving. Unless properly covered you may be forced to buy a more expensive policy at the Customs, or return home.

**NO PANIC ABOUT DRIVING ON THE RIGHT**
Even on your first trip it is easier than you might think. The influence of other traffic helps to keep you "right" but you need to be more alert on empty roads. A passenger who occasionally shouts "Keep right" helps in the first hours and days. Plan to arrive in daylight. Especially if you are alone, repeat to yourself for the first few hours "Keep right" and have a post card with these words facing you on the dashboard. Be extra careful on entering or leaving roundabouts where one is apt to go wrong. You turn right into roundabouts.

It is if you forget this keeping right that can be dangerous. The most likely time for forgetting is when trying to find your way, or if you are on a long clear road and suddenly meet someone coming towards you. In the latter instance, instinct is apt to take you left. So, you must prepare your mind by repeating "Keep right". Get your passengers to help by navigating for you and calling out if you stray from the right. The risk of forgetting diminishes after a few hundred miles until you get home—then, you have to tell yourself to "Keep left" but that is easier.

No one wants to be confused with hundreds of detailed notes just before setting out on holiday (or business) and I think all you need worry about are the few *signs* and *principles* which differ from British practice.

## DIFFERENT PRINCIPLES
### Parking

Continentals rarely stop on the road side. Outside towns there is almost No parking except *off* the road on the verge out of danger. How sensible! In towns and villages pavement parking seems the general rule or in clearly signed wide roads.

### Priority to the Right

Less worrying and more sensible than some people concede, the rule "priority a droite" applies especially on minor roads. Note that anyone approaching on a road to your *left* has to give way to you; thus your prime concern, without dismissing the left entirely, will be to focus attention on the road(s) to your right, giving way as required. The Continentals make great use of this law. The first time someone shoots in front of you from the right can be frightening, but you get used to it!

On the trunk and main city routes this principle is overruled *as and where sign posted*. Out in the country sign No. 1, Fig. 44 appears before each junction coming in from the right, to remind you that your main road is given priority. In villages or towns sign 2, Fig. 44, is frequent and has the same meaning. As a confirming reminder, if in doubt, you can often see the give-way or stop sign facing the incoming road at the inter-section before you reach it, or a thick stop line painted against them.

By these signs the important roads retain priority most of the time but you must impress on your mind that if you suddenly come upon an area *where such signs are omitted*, or if you leave the main route, THEN PRIORITY REVERTS TO THE RIGHT and it's your job to watch it!

Where two trunk roads *cross*, sign 3, Fig. 44, strategically

All these signs have red borders, except 7, which has a white background, no border, and a shaded horn crossed out by a blue line. The key numbers are referred to in the text.

Fig. 44. Some Continental signs.

## ALTERNATIVE NO ENTRY SIGN

Look out in parts of Europe for a different NO ENTRY sign that is occasionally used, if a restriction is temporary, instead of the familiar one (which is the same as ours). It also is circular and of about the same size. The border or rim is red but the whole inside of the circle formed by the border is white and completely blank. Remember – NO ENTRY!

placed to warn you in time, is one YOU MUST REMEMBER because, as the roads are of equal importance, PRIORITY TO THE RIGHT APPLIES.

Equally, on the minor roads you are well signposted to give way at main roads and to allow priority to the right at all others. (Similar give-way and stop signs to ours and sign 4, Fig. 44, or at more dangerous junctions, sign 5.)

*On roundabouts don't forget to give way to the right* in addition to circulating the "wrong" way, i.e., to the right. (You give way to people joining, which is the opposite rule to ours.)

## Policemen

Pass in front or behind them as appropriate. They seem less tied to the rule book than their British counterparts, although they may carry guns!

## Hooting

Over much of the continent *no hooting* is allowed in the towns. Sign 6, Fig. 44, page 169 will be noticed somewhere on the outskirts to tell you and sign 7 ends the prohibition as you leave the city.

## Honk! Honk!

Just as our lorry drivers flash headlights to tell anyone overtaking them they are clear to move in, in Europe the technique is a loud blast or two on the horn. This is a little shattering if you don't know to expect it.

## DIFFERENT SIGNS

Most continental signs are placed on the right hand edge; they are rarely duplicated on the left as in Britain. Figs. 44, 45 and 46 show the important ones which differ from their British equivalents.

## OVERTAKING

To help you, *be sure to have a well adjusted left wing mirror.* It assumes life-saving importance in right hand driving.

One has to lie considerably further back to get a preview for safe overtaking but a few tricks help. When someone passes you and is beginning to overtake the lorry in front this usually

171

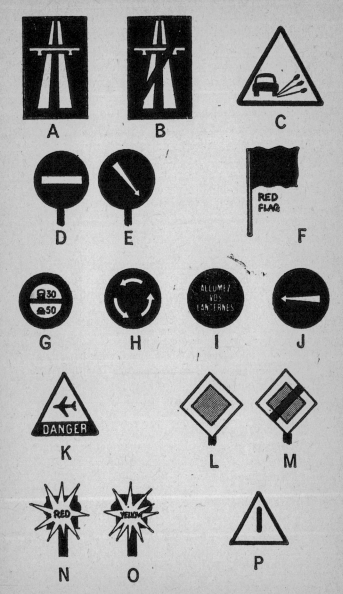

Fig. 45. More European signs. Key to this figure is on page 174

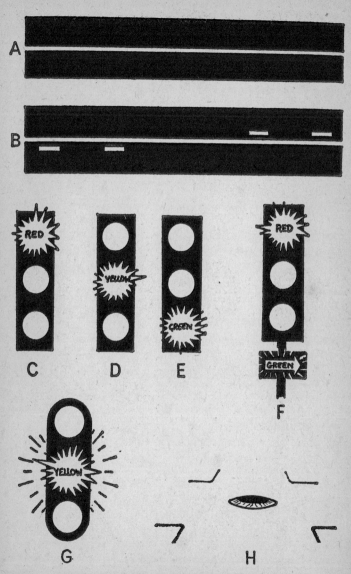

Fig. 46. Continental traffic lights, "bollards", "double" lines.
Key to this figure is on page 174

affords protection for you to move out for a look, if not a "follow through" overtake.

In your mirror, you may see someone overtaking a few positions behind you. This probably means the overtaker knows the road is clear a long way ahead. Provided he has not caught up with you, and is not catching up very fast, here may be a chance for you to gradually move out and look.

The idea is offered at your own risk and care is needed not to cut in front of the overtaker behind you. You may also lean over in your seat to increase vision and make sure it is safe.

A passenger—who can drive—can be of help by telling you the position.

---

**Key to fig 45.**

A—motorway, B—end of motorway, C—loose chippings, D and E—placed side by side as shown mark the start of a dual carriageway, F—temporary danger, G—lorries 30 k.p.h. and cars 50 k.p.h., H—roundabout; arrows remind you which way to go round, I—white letters on deep blue circle show obligatory rule; this example means put lights on, J—turn in direction of arrow only, K—you are approaching an aircraft runway; watch for a flashing alert signal, L—yellow box means start of priority road, M—end of priority road, N—red flashing light; danger and you must STOP, O—yellow flashing light; unspecified danger so slow and take care, P—hazard of some kind; may be specified by wording underneath.

**Key to fig 46.**

A—a single unbroken yellow line equals the British DOUBLE white line.

B—a broken line alongside the continuous one means you may, if safe, cross from the side with the dotted line while it lasts.

*Traffic lights*

C—red, STOP

D—yellow BY ITSELF announces red just coming.

E—green, GO.

F—green filter arrow; you may turn right BUT TRAFFIC FROM YOUR LEFT, PASSING THROUGH THE LIGHTS *on green* HAS PRIORITY; be very careful.

G—*Flashing* yellow: used during quiet periods to save traffic waiting unnecessarily at red if nothing comes. The junction is treated on the basis:— priority to anyone on your right but keep going (with care!) otherwise.

H—Flat circle about 3″ high and 18″ across, lit up at night. Treat like a bollard. You keep right of it just as you keep left of British bollards.

# 14

# Miscellaneous Motoring Knowledge

### REMOVING WINDSCREEN ICE

Quickest de-icer is a plastic scraper—free at many garages—and it never runs out! To prevent washer fluid icing with blinding effect as it reaches the cold screen during arctic weather a little de-icing fluid in the water is almost essential. (Radiator anti-freeze must not be used.)

### GUM BOOTS

Heavy boots, gum boots, or muddy or wet shoes are all murder weapons. I urge anyone to resist the temptation to drive with them. In emergency, one slip—of half a second—may matter. If the soles of your shoes are wet, dry them on a rag or even a newspaper, to prevent their slipping off brake, clutch, or accelerator.

### WINDSCREEN WIPERS

After 5 minutes polishing the windscreen, never forget to wipe the wiper blades free of grease. Wipe indicators, brake and side lights and headlamps while at it.

### DISABLED DRIVERS

Superb advice and assistance is available from Automobile and Industrial Developments Ltd., Sydenham, London, S.E. 26. You need only write, or phone 01-778 7055 stating your particular requirements.

### TYRES

Legislation on the healthy state of tyres can be summarised thus:

Tyres must all be suitable for the vehicle and use made of it; e.g. tyres may need to be heavy duty if a vehicle such as an estate car carries loads. Air pressures must be maintained correct and you can be in default of the law if any tyre is worn to less than one millimetre depth of tread. *More* than this depth must show over at least threequarters of their width all round. No bulges or slits in the side wall are allowed, nor are cuts of more than one inch across the tread area (or of more than 10% of the tread width) permitted if they are deep enough to affect the basic body cords. Any cord showing renders a tyre illegal.

The front wheels must have both tyres of the same type (as must the back ones) and the fronts must not be radial ply unless those on the back are too. Radials on the rear wheels while cross-ply tyres are on the front are permitted, though discouraged.

Advanced drivers would not mix types of tyre on one car at all, except perhaps during a period of changing over, because it leads to having thinner tread on the front than the back. Responsibility of the front for about 80% of braking as well as for steering and, on front wheel drive cars, for motive power is the reason.

The pattern and condition of both front tyres ideally needs to be the same, and both should be at least as new as, if not newer than, the back two tyres which again should be as new as each other.

It is mad to take risks with tyres and wiser to replace them too soon than to take chances. The legal minimum of 1 millemetre is very thin indeed. 2 millimetres would be a more realistic law and advanced drivers would probably want to be rid of old tyres even before they were worn to that level.

### New Tyres

New tyres need to be "run in" for a 100 miles or so for the best chance of long life. It is rare but occasionally happens that a new tyre "bursts". My view is that the inner beads, or edges, need time to settle snugly around the rim. After a "running in" period this should have occurred or any leakage or fault will have had the chance to show. Examine and re-check pressures after 100 miles of careful motoring.

### "Plugged" Tubeless Tyres

Tubeless tyres are often repaired by "plugging" the puncture hole with a piece of rubber glued in. Doubt has been cast as to the long term safety of these repairs and it is strongly recommended that they be vulcanised (congealing the plug and original rubber together by heat) as soon as possible.

If you fit a tube instead of mending the hole it is essential, and garage mechanics may need reminding, to check that all the inside surface of the tyre is smooth. *Rough parts may puncture the tube.*

### Damage to Tyres

Biffs against kerbs, etc., *even at parking speeds*, can cause bursts months and miles later due to unseen inside damage worsening with the flexing of the tyre in use. The sides of a tyre are extremely thin anyway; feeling the thickness of a discarded tyre will shock anyone who doesn't realise this. For the sake of your life have any tyre which has hit a kerb removed and checked. I feel the manufacturers should be forced to make the walls of tyres stronger.

Another point few realise is how easily the "track" or alignment of the front wheels can be upset with consequent tyre wear. Fine adjustment of the track ought to be checked after any knock. It costs only shillings. Excessive tyre squealing at corners is one sign of bad misalignment.

## NURSING YOUR CAR

At least *some* mechanical understanding helps a driver marry his methods to the needs of his car in sickness *and*, in health. For the novice mechanic two other titles in the Paperfront series are a godsend: "Car Repairs Properly explained" and the slightly more advanced The "Car Doctor A-Z", both by B. C. Macdonald. Car "sympathy" as it is often called should be an integral part of a Very Advanced driver's professional approach.

Few things irritate an advanced driver more than when his engine misbehaves and no garage seems to be able to cure it. My experience has been that if you make sure the following are meticulously attended to on an ordinary engine you have little trouble:

1) Plugs. Clean and reset gaps each 5000 miles, renew at 10,000.

2) Contact Breaker Points. Each 10,000 miles renew the

points, setting the gap with fastidious accuracy. Leave *well alone* otherwise.

. Carburettor(s). Only set them yourself if expert; *make sure the job is done only when* (1) *and* (2) *have just been done*, and, apart from topping up the piston dampers if appropriate, LEAVE THEM ALONE. They will quite happily cover 20,000–30,000 miles without any fiddling and the setting *doesn't* change by itself!

(4) Modern "Throwaway" Air Cleaner elements. Turn round so a new surface faces incoming air at 8,000 miles, replace at 16,000.

\*　　\*　　\*

## CONVOY DRIVING

Suppose half-a-dozen carloads of your friends are setting off for a day out. The fastest car should be at the rear and the others arranged in order to the slowest at the front. This helps the back drivers of a fast convoy to keep up, and to catch up should they be left behind bunches of traffic which those ahead have already overtaken.

If possible agree on stopping places in advance if the journey is long. One good way is to plan that the stop shall be within the first mile out of town "so-and-so". Then all know where to look if you have been split up. The first to stop must choose an obvious and safe position which gives the others plenty *time* to see and pull up—then off the road with all the cars if possible.

To enable an unplanned stop to be made (for obvious reasons!) a flash or hooting code so that the back marker could pass a message up to the front is good. Let the message percolate to the front man; he then chooses the next safe opportunity. Discuss these points with your friends before you start. Never allow your convoy to hold up other traffic trying to pass.

## TEACHING DRIVING

Despite the lobbying by those *financially concerned of course*, to make non-professional driving instruction illegal, and their partial success with the passing of the law which makes it illegal to teach for payment unless qualified by a Ministry of Transport test, it is still a fact that of those who *pass* their "L" test about the same number have been taught by friends or relations as have been near driving schools.

My earlier book "Learning to drive in pictures" (uniform with this volume) gives the novice a complete knowledge. The way to learn is set out in logical sequence, bearing safety in mind. The "Driving Instructors' handbook", another Paper-front, shows *how* to teach.

### Emergency stops

The basic reaction "both feet down" (brake and clutch) needs to be taught during the first few hours of tuition. It is for reaction speed that the learner will be tested and which in a "real" emergency can save life.

Technically the clutch should not go down immediately unless the emergency occurs at very slow speed, but it is madness to confuse the first day "L" driver with a twofold rule such as "brake first—clutch down at the last second". In early days a straightforward unambiguous rule is vital.

The quicker braking possible without pushing the clutch down is only by a tiny margin—an advantage which would be eclipsed by a fraction of a second of reaction speed being lost by uncertainty of what to do.

Many instructors and also the Ministry of Transport refuse to accept this argument. In my view the wrong teaching which they advocate about emergency stops is thoroughly dangerous.

Readers who put their hand to teaching must decide who is right.

# *Road Sign and Regulation Idiocy*

Much excellent work is achieved in the advancement of safety by the Ministry of Transport, by Council engineers and others among whom deserving particular credit belong the majority of Police. Regrettably, with little space left I cannot record particular good works without omitting criticism which I hope may be considered, and so this chapter may appear biased towards criticism.

Britain has gone sign mad. We have too largely followed or added to bad overseas patterns. I am certain our excess of signs, by diverting *attention* (particularly speed limits where applied absurdly) and causing over-familiarity, is *increasing* danger especially at night. Not one in 10,000 people remembers the meaning of all these signs, duplications and variations. Many are incomprehensible without previous memorising. Few people bother with this as has been indicated by a number of newspaper surveys. There were nearly 8,000 new traffic orders in one recent year. One must be mentally robust to withstand them all!

I think at least one third of our signs are superfluous and that many could only have been invented by people lacking road-sense and commonsense. Let me give a few silly signs, (see Fig. 47) from our Highway Code and show how they could have been improved.

## IS EMOTION, BASED ON HORROR OF MOUNTING ROAD DEATHS, ASSUMING THE ROLE OF A LEVER FOR POLITICAL ENDS?

That the "things are being done about roads" image helps a Government in power few would disagree. Grand plans are about as important as results, in the race for votes. Anything

This sign formerly had the words NO ENTRY in the rectangle. These should have been kept as even foreigners understand 'NO'

No waiting sign ——— why not? ——→

No passing sign, It could more easily be taken to mean 'pass here' ———why not? ——→

Coaches prohibited ——— why not? ——→

Who would believe ——→ and that this means, that this means 'no cycling' 'you must cycle here'

Play street ——— why not? ——→

No pedestrian sign is right; how could the MOT madmen get all these others so wrong?

The MOT madmen really won here! Beware of airborne motorbikes presumably?

Fig. 47. Silly British signs.

which rouses emotion is wonderful, witness the Breathalyser and the "spy-in-the-cab". (Both the anti-lorry driver vendetta and the drink legislation, as I shall argue, have doubtful benefits to the community as a whole.)

The political game also seems to include extracting maximum taxes from motorists to be squandered largely on anything but roads. If a driver, frustrated and upset by some ridiculous rule, breaks it, laws can make sure he is punished severely. The M.P.'s, presumably hoping to win votes from non-drivers, appear happy to see more and more regulations threatening the motorist. Meanwhile millions are disillusioned by promises of roads to come while frustrated by the collapse, jamming, and disrepair of those here now.

Many well meaning and honest men within the Ministry of Transport and equally uncorruptible policemen are undoubtedly being relegated defencelessly to becoming simple tools in the legalised political horse-trading.

### Drink and Driving

Road deaths since the breathalyser came have crept back to previous levels but this would not seem to rule out some beneficial effect because the number of cars and individual mileages driven have almost certainly increased. *But why attack the motorist alone?* Most drinking drivers knew it perfectly well and could be seen to drive slowly and carefully home. What seems to have escaped notice is the number of drunk *pedestrians* who have stepped out and caused accidents. They are left alone until *found* in a disorderly state. No breathalyser test for them!

The post-breathalyser phenomenon of a man gulping large quantities of liquor when, if not BECAUSE, he knows he has a lift, contrasting with religiously eeking out one or two drinks when it is his turn to drive, has turned the previously regular, even distribution of drinking for many men upside down. Now the urge for bursts of heavy drinking, beforehand eschewed on account of danger when driving home, has been introduced by the new insidious habit of several seeking merriment while one agrees to take a turn at the wheel sober. Sadly the young are most prone to this new way of life.

Who knows where this will lead? How much pain will be felt when alcoholism—born of the breathalyser—takes its grim toll of present day parents to the coming generation? Since the breath test we have seen a gigantic increase in alcoholism. Points to ponder.

### The Poor Lorry Drivers

They (and their bosses) are being attacked with such vengeance, being made to look such rogues, one can easily be excused for assuming there may be some emotion backed conspiracy. But where is there any evidence they have any more accidents per mile than any other group? None has convincingly been cited. The truth is probably as experienced drivers are almost universally agreed, that they are among the finest drivers in the world. The new heavy lorry driver test is rank poppy-cock giving more jobs for the boys. Simple effectiveness of heavy insurance premiums in sifting out the bad drivers has been ignored with the usual cavalier disregard for anything remotely resembling reality.

In my view the whole thing was a political trick to force private enterprise road transport into bankruptcy to enable British Rail and British Road Service to collar the market. Costs don't matter to these nationalized groups.

### Another Blunder

Vans—even the mini-vans—are not allowed side windows because of purchase tax rules, not even slits. If the Minister of Transport was made to drive a van round London this law would quickly be overruled and van accidents would tumble from their present ridiculous level. I ask bluntly, does the average Minister of Transport care about accidents or is it just publicity he craves?

## TURNING FROM BLUNDERS HERE TO BLUNDERS COMING

The results of hard work by traffic engineers can be seen everywhere but if one looks at projects becoming completed daily, despite impressive engineering qualifications, they seem as a body to be moving further from commonsense. Partly I'm sure, the dead hand of bureaucracy encourages and upholds bad design. Let me examine a few examples.

A disproportionate number of accidents statistically involve not vehicles with each other but crashes into solid immobile structures by one vehicle—like lamp posts, trees, traffic lights, bollards and telegraph poles. All can be and are killers.

And yet today lamp posts go up daily in unimaginative deadly positions. It would not be beyond technicians to hang lights centrally on wires, in all but a few places, using buildings or with the poles set 30 feet back off the road; the same applies to traffic lights and telegraph poles. Why not put the phone wires underground?

Trees are being planted . . . and nurtured . . . on central reservations, roundabouts and beside roads—two friends of mine were killed recently when their car hit a pair of 4″ diameter saplings so God help those who hit anything bigger.

One could go on but are we all mad? What kind of escapist passion is it that *will not recognise* cars DO skid, drivers DO make errors, tyres DO burst, and insists (if only by default) in NOT allowing maximum room for these things to happen? Why do we need mammoth right-angle kerbstones to bounce cars back into each other in situations where one driver gropes for the safety of the verge out of the other's way? I don't ask . . . I declare it . . . a lot of our bureaucrats are crackers!

The argument you should not come off the road anyway is crazy. Ministries and councils should call in the advice of drivers who have done at least one million miles of accident free motoring.

Fig. 48 gives an artist's impression of a new roundabout on

Fig. 48.  Badly designed crash barrier.

the M.3 as you reach it. The great crash barrier in the middle masks anything coming round the roundabout. The good sense of restraining cars out of control has been eclipsed by the daft way traffic has to pile up (sometimes literally) before it can see itself safely on to the roundabout. At least 80% of the stops caused could have been avoided simply by designing the barrier with vision in mind.

Entry slip roads on motorways and elsewhere are being built at an angle to the carriageway of about 25–30 degrees. This means drivers have to crick their necks to see themselves safely on to the inner lane while at the same time trying to build up speed and watch out for someone in front stopping unexpectedly. Many with fibrositis have to risk using mirrors alone. A 45 degree angle, by contrast, would not prevent adding speed and would enhance vision immediately.

Another idea relatively cheap and effective for the engineers would be giant spotlights mounted high up for some of the pitch dark junctions between small roads and high speed duel carriageways. These are most commonly really dangerous just beyond the outskirts of big towns after the road leaves the lit urban area and drivers keep belting along plunged in darkness. Accepting that drivers *do go too fast and close to each other*, spotlights would focus their attention on the peril and show up waiting or crossing traffic.

\*     \*     \*

## CONCLUSION

I hope even readers who may have been dismayed by my style of writing will have been able to look beyond it at the larger points discussed. I have tried to make this book about a serious subject nevertheless readable and jolly but I apologise if the method proves in any way discouraging to a reader. Any who are interested in teasing odd points further, or raising issues not examined, or who have criticisms, who wish to write to me care of the publisher, are welcome and I will do my best to help. Please enclose a stamped addressed envelope.

## PLEASE ADVOCATE, AND PRACTISE, THINKING AND ADVANCING!

It is thinking that is needed and not only at the Ministry of Transport!

\* \* \*

### Permission to quote

While this book is strictly copyright the publishers are pleased to allow anyone to use a total of up to five (5) pages from it without asking permission, provided acknowledgement is given thus:

*"From Very Advanced Driving (35p) by A. Tom Topper (Elliot Right Way Paperfronts, Kingswood, Surrey, U.K.)."*

# INDEX

# MOTORING LAW A - Z

By J. L. Thomas

So numerous are offences that can be committed by motorists that they are to be found in this book under every letter of the alphabet except 'X', and for any motorist it would seem to be only a matter of time before a Police Officer has cause to speak to him about some alleged offence. It could well be 'speeding'. possibly the more serious offence of Dangerous Driving, or perhaps some obscure contravention of the Construction and Use Regulations of which there are well over one hundred.

A substantial fine may be the result but more serious for many motorists, the Driving Licence which represents their livelihood can be snatched away by the 'totting up' of three endorsements or by the tell-tale Breathalyser.

A motorists needs to know about these traffic laws to help him avoid their many pitfalls. They are set down here in precise but easy-to-understand language, together with potential defences and much other valuable guidance, by an expert. Former Police Superintendent J. L. Thomas, besides possessing vast experience in all aspects of traffic (including many years as a Court Prosecutor), is the author of six Police legal textbooks, including *Road Traffic Law* and *Road Traffic Cases*, and numerous articles in legal journals and he has frequently broadcast in BBC motoring programmes.

*Uniform with this volume*

# THE CAR DOCTOR A-Z
## Symptoms-Causes-Cures

## *UNIQUE!*

This book is an astonishing A.B.C. fault-finder. Look up the symptoms and the book tells you the causes and cures. Precise step-by-step details of the action to take in every circumstance, routine or emergency.

**NO DRIVER SHOULD BE WITHOUT THIS BOOK**

**YOU CAN SAVE £££s IN GARAGE FEES**

**Behind the book stands our GUARANTEE:**
Return for full money refund if you disagree this is the world's greatest book on the subject.

Many readers will want to secure the same author's companion volume, CAR REPAIRS PROPERLY EXPLAINED. This covers maintenance and explanations of how a car works and used alongside "The Car Doctor" will be of enormous help to the reader.

Also available by B. C. Macdonald :
**BLMC Morris Minor 1000 Repairs**
**BLMC Mini Repairs**
**BLMC 1100 and 1300 Repairs**

Each written with Macdonald's unique analytical step by step approach

*Uniform with this volume*

# PAPERFRONTS

All British Quiz Book
Begin Chess
British and other Jokes
Progressive Brain Teasing Quizzes
Newman's Joke and Story Book
Sample Social Speeches
Persuasive Speaking
Begin Fishing with Uncle Bill
Technique of Freshwater Fishing
Technique of Sea Fishing
Places to Fish in Britain and Ireland
The Fish we Catch
The Best Man's Duties
Wedding Etiquette Properly Explained
Choosing a Wine and Wine and Cheese Parties
Cocktail Party Secrets
Easymade Wine and Country Drinks
Business Letters, Contracts and Etiquette
General and Social Letter Writing
Right Way to Play Chess
Darts
Use a Camera
Dressmaking in Pictures
Golf Secret
More Golf Secrets
Keep Pet Fish
Right Way to Keep Dogs
Horse Keeper's Encyclopedia
Make Money in a Shop
Conduct Meetings, Conferences, Discussions
French English Crosswords
More French English Crosswords
Exam Secret
Help Your Child at School
Improve Your English
Become 200% Fit, Strong and Healthy
Home Medical Encyclopedia
Learning to Drive in Pictures
Car Doctor
Car Repairs Properly Explained
Mini Repairs (BLMC)
1100-1300 Repairs (BLMC)
Motoring Law A-Z
Car Driving in Two Weeks
Driving Instructor's Handbook
Freedom and Reality (Enoch Powell)
Guilty Madmen of Whitehall

*Obtainable from all good booksellers, or, if difficulty, send direct.*

*Uniform with this volume*

**ELLIOT PAPERFRONTS, KINGSWOOD, SURREY, U.K.**